THE SEEDS OF AMARANTH

BOOK THREE

RESUMING THE ETERNAL LEGACY

Heather Charnley

Copyright © 2016 Heather Charnley

Seeds of Amaranth
Resuming the Eternal Legacy

**Copyright
© Heather Charnley
Purple Spirit
Press 2016
ISBN 978-1-907042-26-3**

Heather Charnley has asserted her right, under the Copyrights, Designs and Patents Act 1988, to be identified as the author of this work.

All rights reserved. No part of this work may be reproduced or utilised in any form, or by any means, electronic or mechanical, without prior permission in writing from the publisher.

This book is dedicated to dear Mother Gaia and all the elemental kingdoms.

**Book cover photography and design
Copyright © Sam L. Rollinson 2016**

HEATHER'S FOREWORD

Seeds of Amaranth – Book 3
'Resuming the Eternal Legacy'

This final book of the Seeds of Amaranth trilogy shows how the Oswestry group builds on their experiences from their visits to Atlantis.

It begins with Sarah and Alyssia's trip back to Lemuria, receiving Galaron's support and they travel to the centre of the Earth to visit beings there, as well as Gaia. They also link to an interesting planet they feel they had lived on originally.

As a result of this experience, the whole group travel with the space beings to experience what it is like on a fifth dimensional planet, what they see and how they feel about it, as well as what they discover. They visit two planets as well as Sirius, which compares with the Atlantean culture and the sources of that culture there.

There is a lot of inner journeying, meditation and insights that the group experience in order to understand what they need to know enough of in order to portray what life could be like on Earth if people's links to nature could become as close as their had.

This trilogy is an inspired journey, a way to experience what it is like to meditate and integrate it into your life, how to link to nature in a shamanic way, and especially to conjure up the atmosphere of Golden Ages from other time periods and the sense of closeness we can have with the real heartbeat of life, and the sense of 'all time' where the boundaries between time periods and dimensions can become blurred, allowing the wisdom and light in again!

LIST OF PEOPLE

Contemporary People & Former Casket Holders
Maraya – high priestess, and member of Moroccan group, lives in Atlantis
Costillo – priest, and member of Moroccan group, lives in Atlantis
Sagario – novice priest, and member of Moroccan group, lives in Atlantis
Danuel – novice priest, and member of Moroccan group, lives in Atlantis
Sarah Blenheim – healer and craftsperson (from Zennor) lives near Oswestry (A. name-Salana)
Alyssia Lacey – artist from Kendal, lives in Oswestry (Astragandaran name-Valana)
Karin Sloane – runs Plas Myrddin, Oswestry
Kenny Kenton – Karin's partner, runs Plas Myrddin, Oswestry
Annie – new neighbour near Sarah's house
Glynda – therapist who works in the shop Plas Myrddin (she took over from Bertha)
Garry – Glynda's partner
Benny – hotel owner in St Davids
Jim – campsite owner at Pistyll Rhaeadr

Atlantean Priesthood Members
Hudlath – high priest from 200 years after than Anchorin's time period
Anchorin – high priest on mountain temple in 12,000BC
Galaron – high priest, temple of Elaharia, north island of Atlantis in 23,000BC and Lemuria
Keirion – high priest, sea temple in 23,000BC, contemporary of Galaron

The Council of Twelve
In Anchorin's time
Zanadar –from Cassiopeia
Gelsior –from Pollux
Aurion –from Sirius
Siral –from Andromeda
Maeron –from the Hyades
Golan –from Arcturus
Gillan – from Antares
Talar – from Betelgeuse
Sikaron – from Castor
Melkior – from Lyra
Salaron – from the Pleiades

The Council of Twelve
In Keirion & Galaron's (from book 3)
Zarhavar – from Cassiopeia
Aurial – from Sirius
Salodan –from the Pleiades

Garden of Eden
Arwena – gatekeeper to the Garden of Eden
The Sentinel group – who tend the Garden of Eden
Anui, Deanu, and Giana – guardian priestesses of the essence in the alabaster pot
Leandra, Elandera & Salandra – elementals of the Garden of Eden

Fairies, Elves and Associates from Atlantean & Present Time Periods
Jadeir – elf, friend of Oswestry group, and went on missions with them
Garalph, Ganor, Staloph & Gemalion – gnomes from Pistyl Rhaeadr
Leannah, Philone, Phairos & Alynda – fairies from Pistyl Rhaeadr
Gadair, Cyaphon, Seilon & Kanas – elves from Pistyl Rhaeadr
Kavanos and Kyphos – fauns from Pistyl Rhaeadr
Garderin – gnome at Oswestry hill fort
Alendrin – elf at Sarah's well
Miara – fairy at Sarah's well

The Spirit World Group
Melendra – chief priestess
Pelaré – counsellor and advisor
Sulaya – seer
Eanaya – healer
Zunela – teacher
Azura – spirit who spoke to Alyssia & Sarah from inside the obsidian tunnel, valley of crystals
Arlando – spirit man in Diorama Peaks guiding Atlantean culture in Galaron's time.

Agartha people
Eilara – being who escorted Alyssia & Sarah to Agartha
Kundara – Agartha leader
Alandana – Agartha resident
Raodhina – Kundara's co-helper
Mimirmaré – Kundara's co-helper
Zephira – Kundara's co-helper
Sanjaré – Kundara's co-helper
Gaia – the guiding spirit of the planet Earth

Verdamaran people	**Reluisian people**
Ramusa	**Leana**
Salusa	**Galaya**
Larana	**Enalda**
Viridiana – guide to Oswestry group	**Siraldah**
The Sentinel – in the 'sky' temple	
Arala Suriya	

Astragandaran people
Aurial (1) three angelic beings who accompany the group to the Garden of Astragandara
Astara (2)
Aurastara (3)
Gloriae – another angelic being who is the keeper of Glorae-astraespheres
The Sentinel – the Sentinel group at the Garden of Astragandara
Galarana –first talked to Alyssia and Sarah, reacquainting them to their home planet
Astragandaran Gaia-being – similar to Gaia on Earth

CONTENTS

Heather's Foreword	P3
List of People	P4
Chapter 1 – Preparing for Embarkation	P8
Chapter 2 – The Valley of Crystals	P29
Chapter 3 – The Confluence of Two Realms	P42
Chapter 4 – Preparing the Ground	P50
Chapter 5 – Journey to Eden	P63
Chapter 6 – The Lore of the Legacy	P72
Chapter 7 – Embarkation to Verdamara	P83
Chapter 8 – Behind Closed Doors	P95
Chapter 9 – The Shining Presences	P104
Chapter 10 – The Garden of Astragandara	P117
Chapter 11 – Where All the Universe Meets	P136
Chapter 12 – The Journey Home	P144
Chapter 13 – A New Beginning	P156
Chapter 14 – The Seeds of Amaranth	P176
An Overall View of the Trilogy	P188

RESUMING THE ETERNAL LEGACY

Chapter 1 – Preparing for Embarkation

There were three figures silhouetted against the western horizon on Oswestry hillfort one warm May evening.
"I'm so glad you persuaded us to venture out, Alyssia," said Karin, "it's a nuisance that we're usually too tired."
"Tired or not, I think we'll definitely make more effort to do this," emphasised Kenny, "it adds lustre to the day, perhaps bring our food too!"
"Well I do have a few biscuits, will that do for now?" laughed Karin.
"Oh good!" responded Kenny, grinning widely, he hugged Karin and made a swipe for one of them, "very satisfactory," he tried to mumble with his mouthful.

Alyssia wandered over to the area she had sensed was Guinevere's room in the castle, on her first visit to the hillfort, and also to Oswestry. She had known Karin for a number of years when they both had lived in Cumbria, making pots. Then Kenny had strode into the pottery shop one day, and within six months Karin had gone south to help him plan the setting up of his shop, Plas Myrddin.

A white mist formed where she was looking. Out of the corner of her eye she could see Karin and Kenny laughing and talking together. The mist rose higher and within that, an emerald green sparkling light sat like a large jewel, on the grass. Alyssia gently edged towards it, hoping it wouldn't disappear. Suddenly a gnome appeared out of the ground and stared at Alyssia. They both looked at each other for a moment as if not wishing to break the spell.
"You can see me can't you?" asked the gnome, though it was more of a statement, and his eye hinted humour.
"I can indeed!" replied Alyssia, "can I help you in any way?"
"I don't know about that, humans aren't usually that helpful," and he drew closer, "they never ask us what really needs to be done, nor to the flowers and trees. So how are they to know?" he stated with a shrug, "my name is Garderin."
"Mine is Alyssia," she replied.
"Ah yes! That group who went to Atlantis, word gets around!" smiled Garderin.

He looked over to Karin and Kenny and shouted a loud hoi! They both turned with a startled expression, and on seeing Garderin with Alyssia, they hurried over.

"I have something to tell you all," announced Garderin, "I have word that a lot is happening right now, Earth changes, and we want your help." Garderin looked at the three faces watching him and looked thoughtful. "I thought there was a fourth person in your group!"

"Yes, Sarah, she has a cottage a few miles away," replied Alyssia.

"Can we get there now?" asked Garderin.

"I suppose we could, who's got a mobile?" asked Alyssia.

"Voila!" exclaimed Kenny; "it's been in my pocket all day."

He gave it to Karin and she dialled.

"Sarah! It's Karin; can we come over? We have a gnome friend, Garderin, who wants us to meet up," said Karin.

"Go on then!" replied Sarah, "you must have smelt the cake I was making."

"Lovely! We'll be there in a flash!" chuckled Karin, "she's made a cake." She stage whispered to the others.

They all headed for Alyssia's car, which was parked on the adjacent lane, and drove over to Sarah's cottage, Ty Bach, just over a mile south of Llansilin, to the western side of Oswestry.

Sarah ushered them indoors and they all congregated in the hall.

"Would you like to talk and eat in the lounge? Or do you have another plan of action?" she asked.

"If you don't mind, I would like for us to visit your well in the garden first," enquired Garderin politely.

"Certainly, follow me folks," said Sarah, leading the way through her kitchen, and outside.

The well shone in the evening light, for the sun had still not yet set, and it would be another half an hour before that would occur.

"Alendrin! Miara!" cried Garderin, intuitively knowing their names.

The elf and fairy appeared and greeted Garderin, and then exchanged greetings with the Oswestry group.

"I've come as we have to link up in order to bring through a new form of energy, as a result of what the group helped to bring in," continued Garderin.

"That Zanadar and the Council of Twelve set up, the new improved starway systems!" added Kenny.

"Yes, I shall explain what we shall do," answered Garderin, he stroked his beard thoughtfully a moment and then the three nature spirits looked at each other intently, exchanging silent thoughts that even the others didn't grasp, for the thoughts weren't verbal, but consisted of whole concepts.

"We shall be looking to linking together telepathically and drawing down that energy from the structures in the starways junction that sits at all the meeting points," explained Garderin, "and ask if you can help, by going to designated sites to bring the energy down there too, using your wands. We can practice by your well, Sarah."

"Pity we don't have our wands with us!" exclaimed Alyssia.

"I could get mine, and perhaps give it a go now, so that at least I get the idea?" asked Sarah.

"That will be fine, we can operate and gain ground this way. Could we start now?" enquired Garderin.

"I'll not be a minute!" said Sarah, and she rushed indoors eagerly.

Garderin and the nature spirits all positioned themselves around the well and focused upwards, linking mentally to the starway junction nearest the Pleiades. Sarah came and joined them, for Garderin beckoned her around the well. She pointed her crystal upwards, as the nature spirits had theirs upwards too. Everyone could see a bright iridescent white light, with a faint image of the three intersecting circles come down into the well. Sarah observed the nature spirits, and pointed her crystal wand downwards when they did, and focused on the energy entering the Earth, linking to the centre, home of the Faery kingdoms. Energy was also sent in the direction of Oswestry hillfort, Pen Craig near Sarah's house, St Oswald's Well on the west side of Oswestry, Castle Mound to the north west of Oswestry where they had all first travelled to Atlantis with Maraya, to Pistyll Rhaeadr the beautiful waterfall to the south west, two forts to the south at Llynclys and Criggion, and a well at Woolston to the south east.

"I think that covers the main local energy points," said Garderin, "this will percolate elsewhere, for I've been in touch with my associates who will help distribute the energy."

He turned to look at Karin, Kenny and Alyssia, while Sarah, Alendrin and Miara joined them.

"I think the best action for you four to take is to keep working at this well, but cast a circle first. It is necessary for most humans to need to do that, whereas us nature spirits can repel and dissipate unwanted energy very easily," advised Garderin.

"I do know we are stronger than we were before our encounters with Atlantis," said Sarah.

"Yes, I can definitely see that," replied Garderin, "but the energies here are so strong and bright, they could easily attract attention far and wide. We need to be sure the energy is guarded while it is coming to Earth."

"How often would you advise us to do this?" asked Alyssia.

"Once every few days, maybe once or twice a week, until you sense it is not required any further," replied Garderin, "now I shall leave you, but not until I've tried some of your beautiful cake!" said Garderin politely, and looked at Sarah with a sweet smile.

"Certainly! We know an elf in Atlantis who loves cakes and biscuits too!" commented Sarah, looking at Kenny pointedly.

"Jadeir! He'll be back for more if you start making cakes regularly, Sarah!" responded Kenny.

They wandered indoors, as Alendrin and Miara declined food and drink, to continue their work outside.

The others sat down, while Sarah and Alyssia brought the expected cake and tea on trays, into the lounge.

"Can I ask what to expect in the world as a result of doing this exercise, Garderin?" enquired Kenny.

"Well! There's a question!" laughed Garderin, "to quite a lot of people there may be little for them to notice, and they might even feel a slight apprehension, but puzzled as to why they feel like that."

"Discomfort at energy change, meaning they'd feel obliged to change themselves, but don't realise it consciously," remarked Sarah.

"Absolutely!" responded Garderin, "however, to those more actively spiritual people, they will begin to notice how more beautiful that nature around them looks, and a greater sense of purpose and joy will come into their lives. It will really happen."

"Do you think we've sorted everything out, and no more greys or renegades to encounter?" asked Karin.

"There won't be any more of them, thankfully," replied Garderin, "perfectly safe!"

"Would you all like to stay for an evening meal?" asked Sarah.

Garderin looked a little concerned. Alyssia noticed and spoke to him.

"Do you have work to attend to Garderin? Should I take you back?" she asked.

"Sorry to be a nuisance, since I asked you all to come here," responded Garderin, "but there are some things I must do, on

return. I would be letting other gnomes down if I stayed on, I'm sorry. I've enjoyed being here, and the cake was lovely!"
Alyssia got up to go, when the front doorbell rang.
"I'll go and see who it is," said Sarah, briskly moving in its direction, while Garderin became invisible.
There was an exclamation when the door was opened.
"Annie! What a nice surprise," exclaimed Sarah.
"I was wondering if you needed anything from Oswestry before the shops close. Are the group here?" asked Annie. She gave a half smile. "Are there any nature spirits here?"
"A coincidence you called. We have a gnome who wishes to return to Oswestry hillfort, as the others intend to stay for a meal, would you come in?" asked Sarah.
Annie entered the room and smiled cheerfully at everyone and greeted them. Garderin had reappeared.
"Garderin. Annie is going to Oswestry!" said Sarah.
Garderin looked pleased, and smiled kindly at Annie.
"Don't worry, I'll take you along," said Annie, "we'd better get going as one of the two shops I'm going to, close quite promptly. Oh! Did you want anything, Sarah?"
"Here's a list thanks," replied Sarah, giving it to her, "will you join us later?"
"Oh yes! I'd love to, thanks," came the reply.
Everyone found themselves wandering towards the back door with murmurs of 'I'd like to see how your vegetables are growing,' or 'I'd love some fresh air.'
They all wandered around outside, while Sarah tended some of her herbs. There was a glimmer of light seen from the corner of their eyes, and everyone turned to see where it came from. A familiar figure stood astride the well with a wry expression on his face.
"I knew you needed something useful to do!" cried Hudlath; "I've brought more copies of the Atlantean codes for you all to practice with."
"Oh, how interesting!" remarked Sarah.
"What will we do with them once we've accomplished using these other sets?" enquired Kenny, approaching the well.
"All will be revealed!" replied Hudlath emphatically, with animation.
"Come inside if you like, we've had some tea and cake, but there's more for us all," said Sarah.
Hudlath looked interested and smiled. They all hugged Hudlath and went indoors.
"Now," began Hudlath, after digesting a portion of cake, and showing an appreciative sign to complement Sarah's baking. "I

shall explain. There are another five sets in existence, and at present I've been asked to show you the first three of those, that is, sets six, seven and eight. They are – 'Integrating Higher Dimensional Wisdom', 'Earthing the Wisdom,' and 'Linking to the Magician Within.' The latter one is the first of the last three sets that have a different vibration about them, the others are preparatory, whereas the last three really begin your allotted work in hand."
Hudlath paused, looked at them all intently, evoking response.
"What is the allotted work?" asked Alyssia.
"Indeed, what is it?" queried Hudlath with a puzzled look.
"Perhaps we find out when we use the cards!" said Kenny.
"Yes, you can only find out for yourself, can't you!" stated Sarah.
"Indeed!" echoed Karin, "why should anyone else answer your own questions?"
"I just wanted to know if there was some pre-planned action awaiting us as previously, or something we all have to find out for ourselves," added Alyssia.
"It's a good enough question, knowing you had that intent in your mind's eye," remarked Hudlath, "as are all your responses. Yes, I think the best thing is to leave these sets of cards with you all, to try them for two or three weeks and let me know how you are progressing, all right?"
Everyone affirmed agreement, and Hudlath handed out three sets each to the four of them.
"Now I must return," said Hudlath, "Anchorin needs some help."
He rose from the sofa, as did the others.
"Please send him my regards," said Sarah.
"And ours!" responded everyone else.
"I certainly will, we shall all be visiting him again soon, no doubt!" Hudlath replied with a hint of a wink.
They all went outside again and Hudlath vanished swiftly as he stepped into the well area.
"He's definitely got either a plan or some kind of idea up his sleeve!" remarked Kenny, thoughtfully.
"Yes, you're right, there," responded Sarah, "he was being a bit of a tease, you might say."
They all chuckled, and with that Miara and Alendrin reappeared near the well and joined in with the laughter.

"I don't think we have a moment to lose," said Sarah.
"Strangely enough, I think you're right," agreed Alyssia, "I don't know in what way, just a hunch."
"Well, that's good enough for me," replied Kenny.

Sarah unpacked her number six cards and examined them. "Their sun and moon combined energies with a six-pointed star will obviously be a catalyst for more integration," commented Sarah.
The others got their number six cards out and began to work on them. They each held a right-brained card for the crown chakra upto the third eye area, for that master gland would respond in a universal way to all the cards per chakra, which would resonate according to the chakra concerned. They worked on all fourteen cards; the seven chakras with left and right-brained cards, for about an hour, and then would compare notes with each other on their results.

Sarah looked around after she had finished, and noticed that everyone else was already alert and waiting for her to open her eyes.
"You must have been having a good session, Sarah!" joked Kenny.
"Too right!" she replied, "but I think it calls for some more refreshments!"
"I'll drink to that!" replied Alyssia.
"When we've got it!" added Karin.
"What are you waiting for, the kitchen's all yours!" retorted Kenny.
"It's your turn, you were the first to finish," answered Karin.
"Ok, I know where the cake is!" replied Kenny.
"I should be making a meal for you, oh dear, all this excitement has put it out of my mind," responded Sarah.
"What do you have?" asked Alyssia, "we could all help!"
"Some veg and rice or pasta, nuts and/or lentils," replied Sarah.
"No problem! But shall we discuss what we saw in our meditations while we are preparing it?" suggested Karin.
"Ok, come on!" said Sarah, and they all went into the kitchen.
"With the crown, right-brained card, I felt energy entering me in an earthing and balancing way," said Alyssia.
"When I tried the crown left-brained card, I felt a sword of energy going down the system. It released something from my throat that held a deep guilt I didn't know I had," admitted Sarah.
"I just felt a deep sense of peace linking crown and base, and I felt a sense of relief," commented Kenny.
"I got quite a bit of what you all felt, but also a sense of a timeless Palaeolithic-style consciousness, deeply linked to nature," explained Karin.

"With the third eye card, I felt there was strong energy, causing pressure at the throat, but as I continued, I was able to work and clear the energy pressure there," explained Karin.

"I felt strong energy scouring away and consolidating the head area," said Kenny.

"I saw a load of psychic matter lifted away, and good energy coming in as a result," added Alyssia.

"I experienced a fountain of white light coming down into my head, radiating light around, and then moving down to the base, it was the left-brained card," explained Sarah.

"I felt strong energy working in my throat when I used the throat chakra cards, removing blockages around the carotid areas, which was quite uncomfortable, but it worked," said Karin.

"I felt much the same, like the energy was coming from the third eye to the throat, and then linking to the solar plexus, higher and lower minds sorting something out," explained Sarah.

"I was guided to surround my neck in indigo and gold light, to preserve the energy, and install new energy and power here," said Kenny, "now please give me that carrot!"

"I felt a good surge of energy, the sort that tingles and sparkles through you!" said Alyssia, "and a clear sense of majestic light and free energy around me, for I was told all blocks could be cleared by karmic agreement."

"As for the heart chakra cards, I just felt a lot of energy coming through to my heart from above," said Kenny.

"I did a bit of clearing of cords here, and then I had a blissful time," explained Alyssia.

"Lucky you! I got the impression of being involved in an Egyptian curse, due to parts going missing in a burial ceremony, in a past life, and I borrowed a jar from another tomb, meaning to replace it later, but didn't get around to doing it in time," admitted Sarah.

"I hope it wasn't me you were burying!" frowned Kenny, "dear me!"

"It might have been me, as I got a lot of back pains as energy was trying to get through, and it did begin to and relieve the thoracic areas, eventually," said Karin, looking at Sarah, "did you take my liver?"

"Oh dear, I've been found out, but glad to say I also felt some peaceful energy finally, so we must have passed the grade," commented Sarah.

"All that solar and lunar energy has certainly been working on integration, as after some more clearing of past life influences I felt the loving energy of the heart at the solar plexus," said Alyssia.

"I felt a lot of peace, and a white spinning force around the solar plexus, as if it was cleansing, and energising itself with all the energy pouring in from above," said Sarah, "I'm definitely redeemed this time!"

"A veritable powerhouse indeed!" remarked Kenny; "I just felt a lot of peace and strong energy throughout my body. I actually did feel that a lot of mind energy was moving from the solar plexus to the head centres."

"I got a zap of energy like the white tornado, a bit like yours, Sarah," added Karin, "also strong, heartfelt peace."

"I think I got the trump card with the sacral, as I sat with lovely strong energy, and could have stayed like that for ages," said Alyssia, gaily.

"You must have been very good, getting all that wonderful energy," joked Kenny, "I just ended up doing some clearing and then felt dozy, such is life!"

"Oh what a shame!" retorted Sarah, "I felt good energy radiating through the lower chakras, suffusing them with love."

"Oh I had some clearing to do from the sacral until good energy from the crown could come in," said Karin, "Kenny and I obviously need to do more homework!"

"Down at the base chakra, I could feel energy radiating between the sacral and base chakras," said Alyssia.

"I just felt the union of opposites, i.e. the crown and base, and resultant energy given," said Karin.

"I saw old heavy energies from Atlantean times at the crown, with intent to siphon off energy and distort reality, then I felt the light coming in," added Sarah.

"That sounds awful. I got a dynamic resonance between the base, throat and head centres, but after some clearing I came clean," finalised Kenny, "ah! Let's get that tea, I'm tired out!"

"It's virtually ready, folks, I'll gather some cutlery," cried Sarah, "help yourself to fruit juice!"

She put a pile of cutlery on a tray, and placed four glasses on it, and put a selection of cartons beside it.

They ate their long-awaited and well-deserved meal, and then sat talking a while. Finally, Sarah looked puzzled a moment and let out an exclamation.

"What's up, Sarah?" asked Karin.

"Well, I'd forgotten completely until now, but as you may know, Annie was supposed to be joining us for tea. I wonder what happened."

"Maybe just as well with us doing the cards, synchronicity!" said Alyssia.
"I'll try phoning her," said Sarah, looking at her clock, "it's gone ten o'clock, but should be alright, and she must have my shopping!"
Sarah picked up her phone and dialled.
"Annie! Are you ok?" asked Sarah with a serious look, "oh, I see, shall I come round for the goods now? Ok!" Sarah put the phone down. "She said she's feeling somewhat off colour, a sudden attack of the sickness bug variety."
"It's time we were going anyway," said Karin, getting up.
"Shall we practice the other two sets and compare notes in due course?" suggested Alyssia.
"Yes, we can do that, you're welcome to come over again when you want to do so," responded Sarah.
"Ok, will do!" said Kenny, cheerfully; "steer clear of the Egyptian stuff though!" and he gave an enigmatic look.
The three of them departed, while Sarah went to collect her groceries.

Alyssia awoke extra early one morning, not long after their evening with Sarah. She had been working on the seventh set of codes, like the others, 'Earthing the Wisdom', which proved to be worthy, and they all felt themselves being tested inwardly, to prove they were well earthed!"
'I hope we can make a start on the eighth set very soon, they are the one's that intrigue me the most,' she thought. She did more work on the seventh set, then arose and wandered into the kitchen.

"Ah! You're up early, Alyssia!" cried Kenny, "no doubt you've been code cracking!"
Alyssia laughed, "oh yes, I'm into the secrets of the seventh set now! I can't wait to try the eighth."
"Yes, we've just got a bit more to do to finish our seventh set. Like you, we can't wait to get started on them. Let's hope we'll get going tomorrow at the latest!"
"Absolutely!" responded Alyssia, "the magic hour approaches!"
"I'll look out the crystal ball," responded Kenny, with his enigmatic look.
Karin soon appeared from the bedroom, having overheard the conversation.
"Sorry to bring you down to earth a moment, but remember we've got that big order coming in, could you help, Alyssia?" she asked.

"No problem, it's all part of 'Earthing the Wisdom', isn't it," smiled Alyssia.
"I think I'd rather shift and sort boxes than all that 'Earthing the Wisdom', it was hard work!" said Karin, "but it had to be done."
"Yes, it was like the final big push, and also a conclusive stage in the whole clearing process," agreed Alyssia.
"It was reinforcing too," added Kenny, "I've had energy zapping around inside my head, feet and everywhere in-between."
"Well, you'll feel like taking over when we get tired then!" said Karin with an appealing look.
"I don't like to disappoint you, but that energy's upped and gone now, back to my usual charming self who needs biscuits to keep me going," replied Kenny, putting out the breakfast plates.
"Might have known, but worth a try!" laughed Karin, bringing over a pot of tea.
Alyssia was making toast, and she looked thoughtful a moment.
"Fusion, that was a word I got in connection with this seventh set, a conclusion to all the previous sets," she said.
The others affirmed agreement, and they ate their breakfast.
Later that evening the three of them were gathered around the living room table again, looking weary.
"I'm too tired to do any card activities tonight," said Kenny, "would anyone like to watch a film I got in the post this morning?"
"What's it called again?" asked Alyssia.
"The Seeds of Amaranth-Recovering the Caskets; it's about four people who travel back in time to Atlantis, searching for caskets to return them to Atlantis' golden period," explained Kenny, earnestly.
"Really! I don't remember a director following us about," replied Alyssia.
"Ho! It's really called 'The Vision of Rainbow Rock', about a man who has a past-life recall of being a shaman, and what he encounters, both in the past and the present time slots," he explained.
"Let's see it!" echoed the girls.
They ventured to the sofa, and Kenny put the DVD in the slot.
"You know, perhaps we should write our story, remember that curious newspaper article Sarah found in the well," said Karin.
"Yes, strangely enough I'd forgotten all about it," commented Alyssia, "why don't we all write our own record of what happened, and we can compare notes."
"Yes I think we should," agreed Kenny, "Alyssia, would you like to be chief scribe, and amalgamate our information into those saleable tomes of wisdom the public are waiting for!"

Everyone laughed, but teased Kenny for being too blasé. Alyssia agreed to do the job.

As Karin and Kenny were kept busy in the shop, for the summer trade was fast approaching its peak, Alyssia began to write what she could recall about the origins of the caskets being discovered, and how Maraya came to join them, before they all travelled to Atlantis. She would then show the others what she had written, and they would offer what their experiences and thoughts were, which could be inserted into the growing text.
Also, the three of them and Sarah began working on the eighth code card set, the 'Linking to the Magician Within', for the next day or two.

One evening, a few days later, found all four of them together, comparing notes about the eighth set at Sarah's house.
"Let's get the information on paper, everyone," cried Alyssia, "so the main points of this set is that conical energy we all found forming over the head like a magician's hat, an Egyptian pharaoh's headdress, and also a cone of power."
"Also, strong power coming in, so we could disengage from Earthly life in the context of clear sightedness," added Karin.
"Don't forget about the iridescent cone energy being formed in the causal body and beyond," reminded Sarah, "and extra auric fortification and fiery energy coming into the head and heart."
"And finally, a lot of illumined energy burning off dross, so that Horus' talk to us, of reversing the polarity to allow light to radiate, would happen," explained Kenny.
"Lovely!" said Alyssia, and began concentrating as she wrote down everyone's remarks as swiftly as she could, before asking another question.
"I'd like to know of everyone's encounter with a spirit shaman, what did you all get?" asked Alyssia.
"I saw a being who came to me and brought a python," explained Sarah, "the snake was friendly, but when a strange being approached, the snake wrapped itself around it at lightning speed, and soon had it dispatched, and after that I was told I could do that action myself."
"We experienced the ability to use energy from that cone of power in order to help plants to grow," explained Karin.
"Yes, those old elixir plants of ours were exploding seeds all over the place whenever we began concentrating on them!" said Kenny.
"So that's what that noise was!" exclaimed Alyssia, "I was thinking there were some very potent spells being cast!"

"We still had to go and make tea manually!" laughed Kenny, "unlike Jadeir, who could get everything to move telekinetically."
"There's time yet, dear," replied Karin, "keep practising!"
"I'll start on that lot there!" said Kenny, casting a mesmerising stare towards a plate of Sarah's biscuits, momentarily.

"Look at this! Come and look at this!" cried a figure with a beckoning hand to Alyssia.
Alyssia found herself walking over a lush green land, and realised it was greener than usual, and there were myriads of beautiful flowers of every shade and hue. She followed the female figure, dressed in white, with long hair, curious as to what there would be to see. On rounding a small group of trees, she saw a well, and around it were a mass of very iridescent flowers that were also very delicate and golden in hue. The well itself was just like a natural pond, with water continually bubbling up from below, and there were four small standing stones, arranged around the pond equally. The lady smiled and disappeared, and then Alyssia awoke, and thought over the dream's contents. She then heard Karin and Kenny's alarm ringing, and she stirred to write this dream in her diary.
"Where are you upto now, Alyssia, with our book?" asked Kenny.
Alyssia was about to pick up her toast, and Kenny gestured for her to take a bite first, so she did, smiling as she chewed.
"I've got up to where all those plants out of the casket grew like crazy when we put the green powder on them, and you came up to see what all the screams were about! And I am just recalling what happened when Maraya came. Can you tell me the details, Kenny?" replied Alyssia.
"I certainly can!" he remarked, and began writing some notes on a sheet of scrap he swiped from Karin's desk. Karin came into the kitchen, saw what Kenny had done and quickly examined the paper to ensure he hadn't taken something vital after all.
"Your take on this, and anything after that would be useful, as so much has happened, I'm sure to forget!" said Alyssia, looking at Karin.
"No worries, we all prepared for Maraya's arrival after Kenny met her, and then Hudlath appeared in the shop," said Karin, "or did he appear before Maraya's arrival?"
"Yes he did!" remarked Alyssia, "actually, a simple, chronological list of events would be useful, if you could both help out with that, would be great."

"Sarah's memory is better than ours, Alyssia!" said Karin, "why don't you go and stay with her a couple of days or so, and we can manage here for now."
"Ok! That would be good, and it may get me going with some more painting ideas too!" responded Alyssia, "I'll phone her shortly."

Alyssia knocked on the cottage door, and then turned to look up at the little fort Pencraig, standing proud on the flank of the hillside across the river, when the door opened.
"Hello dear! Lovely you can stay!" cried Sarah, and when Alyssia handed her a bag of food supplies, Sarah exclaimed happily.
"Let's get some lunch, it's all prepared, and then we can get down to business," exclaimed Sarah cheerfully, "outside suit you?"
"Sounds lovely!" responded Alyssia, and she left her belongings by the lounge door, bringing the notebook outside with her.
"Cheese and salad, veggie pate or vegan cheese and pineapple?" asked Sarah, with a flourish of her hand towards the table.
"I'll start with the pineapple one," responded Alyssia, "very exotic, and I like the strawberry edging around the plate."
"I thought about having cherries all over, and cascading onto the lawn and the full works, but decided to be sensible!" Sarah replied animatedly, with a wry expression.
"I wouldn't have minded if you hadn't been sensible!" laughed Alyssia.
Alyssia opened her notebook after they'd eaten.
"Time to behave now and get down to some work I see!" smiled Sarah.
"Yeah, if you could help me get the order of events, I can get going with it all," explained Alyssia, "have you been up to Pencraig fort yet?"
"Yes, but only once so far," replied Sarah, "fancy a stroll later?"
"I do indeed," replied Alyssia, "now! I've got upto when Maraya arrived on the scene."
"Yes, she escorted us on our first trip to Atlantis, while Kenny stayed behind, and we flew across, and had that healing so we became clairsentient," commented Sarah, "Then we went to Pistyll Rhaeadr, and I heard from Rhianah, then Kenny went with Maraya to Atlantis, and exploring codes beforehand, he returns with Jadeir, the visit to Anchorin's temple, and then we discovered where the third casket was."
"Was the Council of Twelve after that?" asked Alyssia.
"Yes and no! That and the casket search happened at the same time," replied Sarah.

"Then Jadeir taught us some self defence with crystals," added Alyssia, "and we practiced at Pistyll Rhaeadr, and the elementals wanted to come with us to Atlantis. I got the message from Maraya's friends."
"Yes, then we heard of Anchorin's trip to the Garden of Eden, and then we went on our trip via Atlantis to rescue the lads," added Alyssia, "is that right?"
"More or less," replied Sarah, "just let me know of any further queries later, as I'm going to have to do a bit of weeding and watering while you write, hope you don't mind!"
"Go right ahead, and I'll get writing here!" replied Alyssia.

Later, as the sun had arced its way past the well, Sarah had stopped hoeing, and was using the hose on all the beds. She looked over at Alyssia and called out.
"Alyssia! Any chance of a pot of herbie?" she cried.
The look of concentration in Alyssia's face took on an air of surprise for a moment, and then she smiled.
"No problem, Sarah!" she responded.
They were soon sharing the pot of tea and some of Alyssia's biscuits she had brought.
"You know, I had a curious dream this morning, Sarah, and because there was nothing hugely dramatic about it, I forgot to tell Karin and Kenny, so I'll tell you about it," said Alyssia.
"Go on, my attention span has increased again after that cuppa," responded Sarah.
"I dreamt of a figure dressed in white beckoning me to see something, so I followed, and we came to a pool that had water gushing up from a spring, and there were four standing stones around it, and the flowers in the area were breathtakingly beautiful, and all the colours to be found were bright and iridescent, like nothing I've seen before," explained Alyssia.
"Well, it sounds lovely," mused Sarah, and then her expression changed, and her eyes became very alert, and she turned to Alyssia, "do you surmise it may mean another visit somewhere?"
"You could be right, Sarah," answered Alyssia.

They wandered up to Pen Craig hillfort, from where they could see Sarah's and Annie's homes and gardens very clearly.
"There's a good view up the valley in both directions, Sarah," exclaimed Alyssia, and she sat down on the fort and looked around. She felt a stirring of energy, running through her, southwards.
"There seems to be a ley energy here, Sarah," said Alyssia.

"Yes, I have noticed, and it runs southwards, though just slightly towards the east, and it heads towards Welshpool," answered Sarah, "I usually am good at finding good quality places to live!"

That night, Alyssia's dream continued with the well, and the four stones around it. The flowers were just as bright, and they had a light of their own, as if illuminated from within. Many tiny beings flew around the flowers, giving them essence to help them grow, and Alyssia smiled and watched them at work for a moment, and then moved away, for the area was surrounded by trees, and she could see a path leading to the brow of a small hill where there was more open ground, and she wished to see where she was. As she proceeded, she could hear music, and the scents from all the foliage greeted her. The sunlight was brighter than she knew it in our time, so the shadows seemed less palpable, and the sky was a pale violet blue shade, which was a contrast with that iridescent spring green colour of the grass. She found herself on the brow of that hill, looking down over a small village, but the houses were made like yurts, for she sensed the climate was mild enough. Accustomed to seeing roads, walls and fences, Alyssia was looking for them, but there were no boundaries anywhere, or any food growing, and the only paths seemed like tracks or footpaths.
'I wonder how they eat?' thought Alyssia, 'or travel, I presume they are still in three-dimensional life, or else they wouldn't have those yurts.'
A smiling face with eyes filled with animation came to Alyssia's mind, and nodded as if to affirm something.
'Perhaps someone is aware of me and my thoughts,' thought Alyssia, 'I hope we can meet up.'
Then she awoke.
'Just when it might have got interesting!' mused Alyssia, 'think I'll tell Sarah, and see what we can make of it.'

"What do you think, Sarah?" asked Alyssia next morning, "it seems as if someone's trying to get through to me, like at other times, when we've both had dreams and meditations. Maybe I'll just have to see if anything else happens and note where it takes me."
"Yes, I think you're right," agreed Sarah, "we don't have enough to go on at present, and we still aren't sure of the time period yet either, past or future, who knows!"
Alyssia gave a look of slight surprise.
"You know, I hadn't thought about the future being involved!"

"Did you bring your wand and Atlantean clothes, Alyssia?" asked Sarah, with a slight smile.
"Have wand will travel is the maxim to have these days!" responded Alyssia, knowingly, "and yes, for some reason I decided to pack my Atlantean gear too, and now we know why!"
"You didn't see what kind of clothing the people wore, or what height they were, by any chance, even though you were on that hill?" asked Sarah.
"No, I couldn't see anyone in the dream," replied Alyssia, "I'll just have to get dreaming again tonight, or we could meditate on it I guess."
"Let's do that," agreed Sarah, "and then have a spot of tea."

They went and sat by the well and concentrated on the image of the well with the four stones. All was silent around them, and even the blackbirds moved away to sing elsewhere, temporarily. Alendrin and Miara appeared to watch them meditating, and talked to each other in whispers.
"Do you think they know what they're meditating about?" asked Miara.
"No, probably not, only us folks know of such places!" replied Alendrin, and they both chuckled genially, looked at each other and disappeared.
Alyssia saw an image of where she had stood on the hill and began seeing herself walking down to the small village, and she came to one of the yurt dwelling places and called out. A figure emerged, and it was the woman she had seen before in the dream.
"Come inside, dear," she said, and smiled cheerfully.
Alyssia went inside, and saw four other women sat in a circle, and to her surprise Sarah was there too!
"You are surprised to see your friend here too, and do you have any idea where you are?" she replied, giving a questioning look to both Alyssia and Sarah.
"In the past, Lemuria?" asked Alyssia.
The lady concerned only smiled enigmatically.
"In the future, though I don't know when?" asked Sarah.
"Sorry my dears, you are both wrong!" said the lady, laughing, "you are both linking to a higher plane, the blueprint of your Earth, and how it really is, your physical world is only one facet of the Earth's reality, and like your physical bodies, could be cast off, and not impede on what happens on the other levels, those levels where most of the real work is done, the Earth plane is just the testing station, though we know how important that is,

but as a whole, from an overall perspective, it is minor in a way, compared with the rest."

The lady ushered Alyssia to sit down, and then proceeded to introduce herself.

"My dears, my name is Melendra, and I am like the chief priestess around here," and she gestured for the others to also introduce themselves.

"I am Pelaré, and I am a counsellor and advisor," said the one sitting next to Sarah, a Hawaiian looking woman with deep magenta clothing.

"I am Sulaya, and I am a seer!" said the woman on the other side of Sarah, tall and slim with Scandinavian features, and pale spring green attire.

"My name is Eanaya, and I give healing," said another with rich blue clothes.

"And I'm Zunela and I teach!" she said conclusively, and she wore bright red clothing with glowing golden stripes.

"I wonder why we were drawn here to see you all?" queried Alyssia, and she looked at Sarah, and then around the room to the others.

"My dears," replied Melendra, looking at Alyssia and Sarah, "you both need to know how life was intended in the beginning."

"And how it will be in the future!" added Pelaré.

"You see, this is the natural state," said Sulaya, "and everyone is so happy and content, and life is simple as no one is trying to cheat or impose on anyone else."

"There is a pristine energy!" stated Eanaya, "which makes for peace, health and good quality of life."

"The inspiration from spirit can enter physical life much more easily," concluded Zunela.

"Excuse me everyone," cried Alyssia, "but how is heaven going to come to Earth? There seems to be too many problems, that it all is anything but heavenly!"

"We know dear," replied Melendra, "it takes effort to see and understand the cycles of life in detail."

"You know what it is like when you drop something on the floor and it goes everywhere, and then you have to clear it up," explained Pelare, "well, think of that on a grand scale, and it's only when people decide they don't want the disharmony and degradation, and take matters into their own hands, that it will really change."

"That seems a lot to consider, as how many people are prepared to actually do anything? Even if they could, we know that governing forces would change the rules to hamper even more!" commented Sarah.

"We know, and that is the greatest challenge of it all," replied Melendra, "how many people would be brave and strong enough to counter the powers that govern your world, the governments, police and armed forces, but the latter are people too, and even they may join your ranks."
"Are we to start a revolution?" asked Alyssia, looking concerned.
They all laughed, and Alyssia could see the sunlight shining on the yurt, creating an illumined patch in the centre of the room, as some of that light permeated the yurt's walls.
"Sometimes these things happen without anyone sitting down to prepare talks or organisations, and it simply is the spirit of the moment at work," explained Melendra.
"Why don't you two go and find out?" asked Zunela.
"You mean, travel into the future?" asked Alyssia.
"Absolutely!" affirmed Pelaré, "you can find out then!"
"Alright, then we will go and see for ourselves!" agreed Alyssia.
"Well, I second that," responded Sarah.
Then they all arose, and Alyssia and Sarah returned home to their own time, eager to tell the others.

The next evening saw the four of them sharing a meal in the flat above Plas Myrddin.
"You mean that we should visit the future?" queried Karin.
"Yes, in order to witness that pristine lifestyle inspired by spirit, and also was present in the very distant past. That's what was intimated," explained Alyssia.
"How far forward and back is required?" asked Kenny, looking quizzically, with his usual shock of curly hair standing proud. He spied a large box from the previous stock buying session, tucked in the corner of the office area, "well that box has to go back, but not into the past! Don't forget to send it Karin!" and he grinned.
"Don't fancy lugging that around, that's for sure!" agreed Karin.
"Lemurian times was mentioned," stated Sarah, with a wry look, "but we don't know for sure how far back that goes, do any of you know?"
"We could ask our friends in Atlantis," answered Kenny, "let's get our crystals into operation mode!"
Alyssia and Sarah brought theirs out of their bags, and Karin retrieved hers and Kenny's from the bedroom.
"Let's all focus on 12,000BC, and Anchorin, and their expressions took on a look of deep concentration.
The evening was quite still, the sky of luminous blues and gold, as sunset approached, and the light was cast into the kitchen where they sat.

An image formed in the midst of their crystals, of a distinguished looking man with long grey hair, and alert, violet eyes.
"Greetings, my friends! How are you all?" he asked, his hand was palm up as usual.
"Greetings, Anchorin!" everyone said in unison, palms up in response, "we are all well, and wish to ask you about when in the distant past the Earth would have been pristine, like it is in spirit?" asked Alyssia, "though we know your time is pretty good."
"Yes it is, but realise what you want to know, the origins," mused Anchorin, and he looked thoughtful a moment, "I might ask Hudlath, as I'm sure he was in touch with some of the earliest inhabitants. I shall summon his presence!"
Anchorin focused on another crystal, and soon enough a faint image of Hudlath appeared, hovering beside Anchorin, just over his shoulder.
"A gathering I see before me!" stated Hudlath, "greetings all!" and he gestured accordingly with the upturned palm.
"Hudlath, my friend, our group needs to know the origins of when life was as pristine as in spirit. Do you know how far back in time they would need to go, in order to visit that time period?"
"Good question!" answered Hudlath, "the only person I can think of is Galaron, the high priest who was and is an expert traveller. Did you not meet him some of you, when you looked for Maraya?"
"Oh yes, I'd quite forgotten his name," said Karin, "yes, that's right. We'll have to recall when his time period was."
"All right, I shall focus on the fellow, and see what he says!" replied Hudlath, who duly focused on Galaron a moment with another crystal, and an even fainter image of Galaron was visible to the Oswestry group.
Hudlath had explained to them on a previous occasion that images of people become increasingly fainter when other people summon them via crystals, when it's in a chain formation like this.
"Galaron, my friend!" announced Hudlath, "you remember Karin and Sarah when they visited Keirion on the northern island of Atlantis?"
"Yes, I believe I do! Greetings to you both! How can I help?" asked Galaron.
They wish to know when the origins of life on Earth was pristine," asked Hudlath, "but they can explain why, if you wish to know!"

Galaron looked at Alyssia and Sarah with intent, and they felt he could understand why just by doing so. As they perceived that Galaron's eyes seemed to acknowledge their comprehension.

"My dears, travel back to my time, and I can talk to you directly, it is well to consider returning to about 27,665BC, but just think of me, my friends!"

Galaron's face faded, Hudlath concluded, and his face duly faded. Anchorin asked the group to let him know how they progressed in their discoveries, and then his face faded as well.

"Are you both happy about going so far back?" asked Karin.

"I don't think it will be anything to worry about! No dinosaurs at that time, eh?" commented Kenny.

"It will be fine," stated Sarah, "Galaron looks happy enough."

"Will our clothes be okay for Lemuria?" queried Alyssia.

"I'm sure they'll be fine," answered Sarah, "but perhaps Galaron can advise when we get there."

"What's happening in the shop tomorrow, Kenny?" asked Karin.

"Ah, appointments in the healing room. We have the new lady starting tomorrow, so not a good day really," shrugged Kenny.

"Oh yes, what's her name again?" asked Karin.

"Glynda, she does crystal healing, as well as aromatherapy and massage," replied Kenny, "and I'm sure that she'll be open to all our activities once she gets settled in!"

"Crystals! Will be useful! We'll travel back at Ty Craig then!" said Sarah, cheerfully, "but not tonight eh, Alyssia!" and she laughed.

"I'll second that!" responded Alyssia.

Chapter 2 – The Valley of Crystals

It was a beautiful sunny, early August morning. Sarah and Alyssia awoke. They both stirred early, somehow inspired to make the most of the day.
"I think we are being inspired to go back to Galaron's time period today, Sarah!" said Alyssia cheerfully.
The light shone through the living room window, catching the side of her face.
"You are right! I had a dream of Galaron beckoning me, and that deep blue clothing he was wearing when Anchorin communicated with him seemed to glow," replied Sarah.
That sounds interesting, because I saw a feather floating past my window when I was getting ready, and for a split second it appeared to be deep blue," commented Alyssia.
"Well, that's settled then, we'll go today!" laughed Sarah.
"Where should we go from?" asked Alyssia, "we'd be spotted by the pool, perhaps?"
"I think so, it depends whether people are looking on the road past Pencraig, or from the farms to the west, who knows. We can go from inside!" replied Sarah, "but link via the well when we depart."
They obtained their Atlantean clothing and the relevant herbs, the elixir to make them Atlantean sized, and the blue mist plant supply too for a quick acting disappearance, just in case.
"Focus hard on Galaron and the year 27,665 years BC!" cried Alyssia.
They both became Atlantean sized, with their crystals glowing, and then they disappeared from Ty Craig and the twenty-first century.
A bright and iridescent shimmering light greeted them, and they found it hard to see, for the light was dazzling. They instinctively put their hands up to shield their eyes, and then managed to adjust to the view that became apparent. They were sitting beside a beautifully cared for well, with extraordinary flowers of iridescent hues, beside and around that were verdant lands, with huge wooded mountains, interspersed with silvery shining waterfalls. When they looked at the well again, they noticed a small stream running from it down to a mirror-like lake, which reflected the images of more wooded mountains, and there were white temples peeping from between the trees.
"Well, some people must live around here!" remarked Sarah.

"Let's look around that corner!" said Alyssia, "I'm sure something of use will be there, like a temple, so we can make enquiries."

Sarah indicated that Alyssia lead the way, and they wended their way around the side of the hill. Sure enough, on a flattened area, halfway up the hill, stood another temple, with associated buildings. They approached the temple and walked inside. It was round, with a domed top, and there was an aperture at the apex of about three feet in diameter. The interior was quite simple, white again, with a fire burning in a central hearth, so that the smoke rose up through the aperture. As their sight adjusted to the comparative shade within the temple, they noticed things more increasingly. There were seats around the circumference and various shrines, including one near the hearth.

"Welcome my friends, we meet at last!" said a voice from behind Alyssia and Sarah.

They spun round in surprise to see the familiar face of Galaron, his animated eyes alight with an ethereal glow, and his robes of deep iridescent blue went down to his feet. He smiled and held out his arms, walking towards them. They greeted him in turn, and they all hugged each other.

"What a beautiful place!" cried Sarah.

"It's unbelievably beautiful, without fences, cars, factories and motorways," said Alyssia, "I wished I'd brought my sketch book!"

Galaron smiled, "Well, now you know where we are, you can visit any time! And yes, we are so much better off without those vehicles, roads and all the contraptions your society has, but you may well wonder how we built our temples and dwelling places, for you are aware that levitation of objects is possible, aren't you?"

"Well, yes we are," replied Sarah.

"But never seen it done," responded Alyssia.

"You will know, once you've spend a night in the Valley of Crystals!" remarked Galaron, giving an enigmatic smile.

Sarah and Alyssia looked at each other with intrigued delight.

"Are they from Earth?" asked Alyssia.

"Some are, and others from Sirius," answered Galaron, "brought by the first visitors to Earth, to ensure blueprints of consciousness could be effectively transferred here. Now! You'll have to experience it for yourselves, my friends!"

"Point taken!" responded Sarah, and they all chuckled.

There was a sound, strangely familiar to Alyssia and Sarah, and it was coming from just outside, over towards the green land nearby.

"It sounds like a spaceship!" exclaimed Alyssia.

Alyssia and Sarah turned swiftly to look out of the temple door, to see the spaceship in question.

"You know who is on it, my friends?" said Galaron, smiling, "Zarhavar, Aurial and Salodan are calling to let me know a few matters."

They all swiftly moved outside and over to the approaching craft, a broadly conical shaped ship that glinted with silver and iridescent colours. It landed gently onto the green land near the temple, and the three space people alighted, and also approached Galaron, Sarah and Alyssia.

"Greetings friends!" cried Galaron, and raised his palms up, just as everyone else did.

Alyssia realised that this Atlantean greeting went back far further in time, and had originated on Sirius.

Later, Galaron escorted the group, including the space beings, around to his private dwelling, and they sat outside as evening approached. The starlight glowed like pearly lights on indigo velvet, Alyssia had thought. They all sat together in silence, moving into a meditative state. A rushing glow of energy came into Alyssia's mind's eye, and grew brighter, reminding her of the sudden effect of the code cards when she was on Oswestry hillfort.

"Be calm! Be still! The mind of the universe is with you, and will be your guide, as it was in the beginning of time on Earth."

Unearthly energy played around them all, looking something like ethereal aurora borealis colours, with the additional colours of silver, pearlescent and golden light. Then it all faded to as it was before. Alyssia and Sarah gradually opened their eyes to see everyone else smiling gently towards them.

Zarhavar indicated for them to look in their upturned palms. To their surprise, a small rounded crystal was sitting in each of Sarah's and Alyssia's palms. They glowed with the same aurora borealis-like rippling of colour change that they had experienced.

"What kind of stone is this?" asked Sarah, quietly, not wishing to break the peaceful atmosphere.

"Glorae-astraesphere is the name, they are seeded from the stars, and were on Earth for a short time, before the levels of the physical realm were sought," said Galaron.

There was a strange humming sound that came from the stones, which Sarah and Alyssia found quite moving, though they said nothing, as their attention was taken with the stones, but the others could sense what was happening.

"Tonight you must go to the Valley of Crystals and take the Glorae-astraespheres with you, my friends," advised Galaron, "the stones will make their own way home!" and he smiled at Sarah's and Alyssia's looks of surprise.

"We must depart now," said Zarhavar, "I know we are wanted elsewhere."

Aurial looked thoughtful a moment, "yes, Maeral, Gelsan and Sikal are calling to tell us we are needed in that neighbouring galaxy again."

"Oh dear, that means trouble, for they are in the Kali Age!" replied Salodan, "it was nice and quiet here, very enjoyable."

"Never mind, duty calls!" responded Aurial.

"And we are doing good work!" they all said in unison, and smiled.

Everyone got up from their seats and exchanged greetings, and they saw Zarhavar, Aurial and Salodan to the spaceship.

As the ship shot up into the night sky, and promptly disappeared into a higher dimensional state, Galaron turned to look at Sarah and Alyssia, his eyes shining like stars, with little points of light moving around in them. "Let us embark for the Valley of Crystals my friends!" he announced.

Swiftly gathering some food in a bag from the table, Galaron led the way across the plain of grassy land towards one of the hills in a recessed area. Alyssia and Sarah were quietly looking around them and at the night sky. It was as if their life in Oswestry was slipping away from them and there appeared to be nothing to talk about, or even remember at that moment. They ascended the hill, and the path trailed along an escarpment to the summit. Once there, they found more hills and mountains reaching ever higher. Galaron indicated a route to their right, which took them through a small pass, up another hill path, then through another pass route between two mountains, and then the path curved around a little to their right again. Galaron stopped there and turned to them.

"We are here now, just walk down between these rocks for a few yards and that is the place to stop. Here is some food, and a rug to lie on will be there for you. I shall leave you here, but you will know how to return easily enough, and when the right time is to do so, after being here. Spend as much time as you need to, there is no time limit! Goodbye my friends," announced Galaron, stepping away. "Oh, and don't forget to hold up your Glorae-astraespheres on arrival!"

Galaron smiled broadly and then disappeared down the trail.

Alyssia and Sarah looked at each other a moment and smiled.
"An adventure awaits!" said Sarah.
"Indeed! Let's get going!" joined in Alyssia.
They both linked arms and walked gently and quietly downwards for a little way, and then the ground levelled out and they came to the designated place.
They wordlessly indicated to each other where it felt best to stop, and two rugs appeared beside them, and they sat down to contemplate the place.
Neither of them felt inclined to speak, but held out their Gloraeastraespheres, which began humming again, and they both fell into a deep trance-like sleep, which was very healing.
Alyssia was dreaming of a small being with a green light around him, calling to her.
"Awake, my friend, the crystals are calling to you, hear their song, hear their song…"
It was like a high-pitched choral song with the elusiveness of Holst's The Planet Suite, of Neptune the Mystic. Gradually, Alyssia opened her eyes, and quickly shut them again, as the light was so bright. She re-opened them again, having shielded her eyes and realised it was still night-time. She was about to wake Sarah, but there was a voice that said, "leave her, and she will awaken when she has been called to do so, in the same way you have been."
Alyssia realised it was the stones that were glowing, and she knew she had to go to them. She held the first she was drawn to visit, and could feel power rushing through her, pulsating and glowing, and a huge eye overseeing the whole energy field.

"Oh child of the heavens, do you remember the time when you lived here? Do you? And beyond that? Where do you come from?"
Energy lifted from the crystals so strongly and rushed through Alyssia, that she was transported to another place. She could see herself living in a temple like Galaron's, and going to visit these crystals periodically, to maintain contact with whom or what? Just then an arcing radiance lifted from the crystals high into the heavens, sending messages out to a destination, though unknown to Alyssia at present. She then felt drawn to go and lie down again and promptly fell asleep once more.
Then it was Sarah's turn, she was summoned to awake, and she rose to see the astonishing sight of glowing crystals. She held onto a crystal column of choice, felt the vast power surging through the stone, and then the same question as Alyssia's, and then she, too, returned back to fall asleep on her rug as well.

Alyssia was flying through the heavens towards a group of bright stars. "Glorae astrae" kept on coming into her mind, and the swirling aurora borealis light encircled around her as she flew along. Sarah was beside her, flying along too, and they smiled to each other, and came to a luminescent, sparkling planet, 'from where the Glorae-astraespheres originated', came the response.

They landed on an iridescent, spring green surface, with lots of golden flowers, with sparkling lights in their centres.

"Like light shining on water," remarked Alyssia.

"Fantastic!" cried Sarah.

They both looked around themselves in amazement at the colours, and the flowers seemed to grow and lean towards them in response to their appreciation. They found other flowers like roses, yet with a pearlescent light bathing every petal, and a moving inarticulate song emanated, accompanied by a perfume that made both of them positively ecstatic.

A beckoning arm drew them over to a mountain, and they found themselves moving at speed underground, along a grand, crystal-lined tunnel. They slowed down in front of a door that had a fairly ornate design on it, etched in green light.

On touching the door, it opened, and a staircase rose up to a starry light. They proceeded, and then there was a mass of dazzling light, and they found themselves inside the structure that was quite transparent, with lots of slightly opaque facets. They were inside a crystal and it was at least twenty feet high!

The Glorae-astraespheres glowed so brightly that Sarah and Alyssia found it hard to hold them steady, and the humming sound rose to a crescendo. At that point, Sarah and Alyssia became so moved that their eyes were streaming with tears. Suddenly, they were surrounded by angelic beings, each with a Glorae-astraesphere crystal that hummed in unison.

"We are at home!" cried Sarah and Alyssia, and the angels nodded in affirmation. Then the two found that energy came around their bodies, emulating the fiery glow of the other angels, and wings of fiery light darted outwards behind them both, and then settled to a radiant glow, and they both smiled in delight.

"Welcome home, my friends!" said one angel, and they all converged together and shared their light. Sarah and Alyssia felt so blissful, they thought they couldn't take any more!

It was sunny when they both awoke, and they looked over to each other.

"Do you remember that planet we went to, with the giant crystal, and the angels?" queried Sarah.
"Yes, I remember, and they all had Glorae-astraespheres, and it was so blissful there!" replied Alyssia.
"I don't recall the planet's name, do you?" asked Sarah.
Alyssia thought a moment, "Astragandara" comes to mind, and it may be something like that," she stated.
That sounds nice, it may become clearer while we stay here. Let's have something to eat," said Sarah.
"Yes, lovely, and then explore around," replied Alyssia, and Sarah agreed.

They wandered down between two crystals that towered over them on the far side of the circular space they were inhabiting. There were crystalline steps that led downwards in a slow spiral, and then they noticed a dark entrance.
"Do you want to enter this place?" asked Alyssia.
"I'm not entirely sure, but we could venture a short way and see," replied Sarah, "what do you think?"
"I'll just put my head inside the entrance and see how it feels in there!" said Alyssia.
She stepped forward, and as she put her head inside, a sound emanated from the tunnel, like a deep choral sound.
"Alyssia!" cried Sarah, "come out! Part of you disappeared."
Alyssia turned around, and somehow found herself unable to move easily, and Sarah had to pull her out. They both sat down nearby, and Alyssia then lay down.
"That was quite disorientating, I wonder what it was all about?" commented Alyssia with a rather dazed voice.
"I think we ought to return to the circle and meditate on it there," advised Sarah, "or, perhaps I can while you rest."
Sarah had to half help Alyssia to rise up and move back up the steps where they then sat down.
"I'll just meditate lying down, Sarah, and we'll compare notes in, like half an hour's time," commented Alyssia.
"Sounds fine to me!" agreed Sarah, and they composed themselves accordingly.

The crystals around the circle began to gently glow, increasing their strength gradually, as their meditation became deeper and more focused.
Alyssia could see the tunnel again, not as a dark structure now, but as a burst of blazing light, and that blackened corridor of obsidian was now a pearly white, glowing with golden sparkles. She asked what its function was, and she found herself rushing

through it and floating along, somehow going downwards, but up into space at the same time.

Sarah could make out the corridor of black obsidian too, and saw its blaze of white light, and then voices were heard, 'come... come my friends, do not fear, I invite you to enter, and all will be well for you both.'
"Who are you?" asked Sarah, telepathically, "the elders invited us to come here."
"That is perfectly acceptable, and you are here to experience the lands under the crystal mountain, there are routes and corridors, unexplored by many, but for now you can enter this small route, and you will see much. That is all I have to say at present, my friend, except that my name is Azura."
They both stopped meditating, and sat in contemplation for a while, before considering that obsidian tunnel.
Sarah turned to look at Alyssia.
"You know when you half disappeared, Alyssia," ventured Sarah, "perhaps that condition caused you to feel disorientated."
"Oh, I know what you mean, if I had totally disappeared, it would have been alright," replied Alyssia.
"Yes, because one part of your body was at a different frequency from the other part, so that was the cause," added Sarah.
"Indeed, my body certainly wasn't coping with the lack of balance that the condition caused," commented Alyssia, "anyway, that makes it more encouraging now for our venture into the unknown."
Sarah smiled, "well, you sound ready! Let's go then!"
"Look!" exclaimed Alyssia, "the crystals!"
Sarah turned to look at the crystals in front of them, and they began to glow again, and the two women felt and saw strong rays of light being directed towards them, flooding them with powerful electrical energy.
"It's like looking into a gyroscope," gasped Alyssia, wide-eyed.
"Down a wormhole to a sun!" echoed Sarah, with a mesmerised look.
They ended up lying down, for the energy was too powerful for them to move at all.

Alyssia's first conscious glimpse was of that starry sky, which reminded them of pearls glowing on indigo velvet. Sarah's eyes were now open, and they both slowly sat up.
"We must have been unconscious for hours!" exclaimed Sarah, and she looked thoughtful a moment, then spoke again, "I feel

different somehow, but not sure how to describe it, do you feel different?"
"Yes I do," agreed Alyssia, "it's like we've been topped up by an unknown energy," and she looked as thoughtful as Sarah, "it seems not of the Earth or even of our own universe."
"You could be right," agreed Sarah, "I'm not sure how you can discern energy from another universe, but somehow I know inside we could well be right!"
"Do you think we are ready for the tunnel of obsidian now?" questioned Alyssia.
"If we don't get stopped by something else, we are, I reckon," answered Sarah.
They stood up, took another bite of their food, and walked slowly towards the path that led down to the tunnel. The circle of crystals merely glowed so gently that they looked faintly luminescent in the evening light. As Sarah and Alyssia passed the ones either side of the path, the crystals shimmered, and a gentle humming sound emanated from them. Alyssia and Sarah just knew that the crystals were linking some wordless message to the tunnel to say that they were coming down the steps. Somehow it was reassuring, and that they were being watched over kindly.

Sarah and Alyssia looked at each other as they approached the tunnel entrance and held each other's hands.
"I don't want you to disappear, my friend!" exclaimed Sarah, "and leave me feeling alone!"
"I'll try not to this time!" replied Alyssia.
They ventured into the dark entrance, and once inside, it ceased to be dark, and became an illumined and lustrous corridor. All sides were lined with obsidian, including the floor, and the ceiling area was curved, and nowhere had any delineated sharp corners, separating the floor from the walls, for instance. Light appeared to emanate from the obsidian, and they examined the detail of the walls around them for a moment.
"If you look at this obsidian long enough, you feel as if your whole existence somehow disappears, or becomes part of it," remarked Sarah.
"I feel like I don't belong anywhere, but somehow to everywhere, everywhere that is linked to the centre of the universes," agreed Alyssia.
Sarah turned to look at Alyssia with an alert, animated expression.

"Yes! The centre of the Universes, for that is where there is the vastness of nothingness, which is something so grand and necessary, and is axiomatic to all life," she replied.
They looked at each other in wonderment, and continued along the tunnel. Each of them knew that the Inner Source would guide them to where they needed to go, within the tunnel.
Sarah then spoke gently, "Alyssia, can you hear that faint melody?" Where's it coming from?"
Alyssia listened a moment and pointed to a part of the obsidian wall. They approached the area and listened, their ears pressed against the cool and smooth surface.
"I feel it's calling us back," said Alyssia, her eyes revealed how moved she felt, but didn't find any words to define her feelings.
"Back?" said Sarah, "you mean we've been before?"
They continued in silence as they were still listening, each now visibly moved by that music, unable to find words to describe what it meant to them, or in general, as it was beyond words, yet they somehow knew the music deep in their souls.

The corridor curved around to the right, and then came to an end. Sarah and Alyssia looked at each other again with puzzled expressions. They searched the area for any hidden doorways, control mechanisms, or anything of relevance to be found.
"Perhaps we should meditate on our next move," said Alyssia.
Sarah sat on the floor as Alyssia was talking, and then indicated for her to sit down as well. As they shut their eyes and focused, a boost of energy charged up the area around them, and part of the wall appeared to dissolve, and each of them saw an image of that dissolved wall in their mind's eye. They felt drawn to come out of the meditation, having become alert at the physical level, got up and went to look through the open space.
"Another corridor, Alyssia!" exclaimed Sarah.
"It appears to be going downwards!" said Alyssia, "nearer Agartha perhaps?"
Sarah gave Alyssia a knowing look. They continued onwards, intrigued as to what would happen next. Some steps had been carved into the smooth surface and led them downwards safely. They then turned a corner, and after a few paces on, there was another flight of steps, and they began to descend them.
Alyssia stumbled and gave a slight gasp, expecting to fall, worried, as the flight was at least fifty steps.
"Sarah!" she cried.
Sarah reached for her, but then Alyssia floated in the air and righted herself, landing on the steps again.
"I didn't do that, Sarah," cried Alyssia.

"I wonder who did!" replied Sarah, "maybe we'll find out along the way."

Once at the base of the steps, there was a wider area, like an antechamber, with several doors. The doors had oriental style arches at their apexes, and were apparent to Alyssia and Sarah as being of the same obsidian finish as the rest of the tunnels and the antechamber area.

"I've never seen so much obsidian!" commented Sarah, "shall we try a door?"

"Maybe we should meditate again and see what happens," ventured Alyssia, "just in case!"

"You're right, we can't be too careful in unfamiliar surroundings, however benign it appears to be," agreed Sarah, "although there is nothing unfriendly here, we need to ensure we understand."

They meditated in the centre of the chamber. Alyssia saw the chamber fill with a blue light, which also illuminated each door in turn. Thoughts entered her mind; 'the first door to the left of the corridor is called..., oh there's a glyph and what does it mean? An eye with a four-pointed star-like shape, sort of, around it, no, it's two-pointed at either side of the eye, with energetic force between the points. The next has another eye with a shape beneath, like an open book in profile. The third is like an open book, held up with a four-pointed star at its top. The fourth and fifth both have keys, and the first has an eye in its door handle, and the second has a four-pointed star, and is surrounded by energy. What do they mean, I wonder?"

She opened her eyes a little to see if Sarah had finished her meditation, so they could compare notes. Sarah was looking at her, so Alyssia told her all she had seen. Then Sarah told her what she had received.

"For door one I got 'The Noble Realm', for door two, 'The Room of Memories', for door three, 'The Words of the Ancients', for door four, 'The Key of the Ancients', and then it stopped," explained Sarah.

"Possibly the last one should have 'The Key' in its title, since I saw a key there. There is also a four pointed star, and for the chakra cards, it was always linked to eternity," smiled Alyssia.

"You have it!" cried Sarah, "The Key to Eternity".

"I think I like that one the most, what do you think, Sarah?" asked Alyssia, "it's just that I think the others may talk of right living and old ways of life, and cultures of previous civilisations."

"Yes, you could be right, there," agreed Sarah, "the culture and noble ways of the ancients are fine, proper and good, but may not be the reason for our coming here, and it may lead us astray. How about if we meditate again on the fifth door, just to confirm our choice?"

"Certainly, it's best to be sure, and we can try and see what we must do to gain entry too," added Alyssia.

Sarah gave a thumbs up, and they concentrated once more.

"Concentrate on the name of Eilara," said a female voice within Alyssia's mind. So she did, and kept repeating it. After a while, there was a stirring of energy, and that strangely dreamy music could be heard again.

Alyssia opened her eyes and looked at Sarah, and they knew they'd both had the same experience. The fifth door opened a crack, and brilliant, dazzling light emerged. It was too bright for them to take, but they were aware of an ethereal figure emerging through the door, calling their names, and beckoning them to come. They arose and followed the figure, who placed herself between Sarah and Alyssia.

"Hold tight!" she said, and they went through the door, and there was nothing there. No stairway, obsidian corridor, or anything else to be seen, except for brilliant light. After the initial shock, they felt that the figure with them was alright, so they should be too, and just went with whatever was happening. They shut their eyes as the light was of a fiery brilliance, but they could both see their companion's face in their mind's eye, smiling.

"I am Eilara, and we are going to Agartha, and you chose the right door!"

"Where would the other door have led?" asked Alyssia.

"The first would have taken you to a room full of old images of warriors, and then you would have had some of them converse with you, and then you would have made your way back up to the crystals. With door two, it would have been another room with many cases of information, so you could play back the thoughts and feelings of many people over the centuries. Absorbing for some, but not for you, and you would have lingered a while, and then made your way back to the crystals. With the third door, the words of the ancients, there would have been much information of wisdom given here, quite spiritually uplifting for many. You could have visited shrines and great halls of knowledge seen in Atlantis, for you would have been able to walk through the door into that world, and talked with kings and priests, and their followers. With door number four, the keys would have given you the insights of the priesthood and priestess-hood down the aeons, and not only from this planet either, the origins of wisdom," explained Eilara.

"So, what will we find at Agartha, Eilara?" asked Sarah.

"Ah! That is something you need to experience, for it cannot be explained very easily. I can try, but it won't cover all aspects, or very satisfactorily," Eilara paused a moment in thought, "being in Agartha is like experiencing everything at once and immediately, all time periods, and yet none, for you can focus on what you want to see initially, but once attuned, all is seen!"

"Heavens! That sounds strange," remarked Alyssia.

"It will need some adjusting to," said Sarah, with a hint of concern.

"People are always helped in this, my friends," reassured Eilara, "we shall reach Agartha in a minute."

Chapter 3 – The Confluence of Two Realms

Through the dazzling fiery energy, there emerged a crystalline domain, sparkling and bright. Alyssia and Sarah could look at everything now with fully opened eyes, without feeling discomfort. Everything was a golden white colour, emanating light. They could see small dwelling places like simple huts, with pathways interlinking them, and a larger group of bigger buildings, one or two of them quite ornate. Then they gently touched down in the midst of them all.

Eilara let Alyssia and Sarah go, and Eilara called out telepathically, as usual, to the people there. Out of the largest of the ornate buildings stepped a group of people, all tall, like the Atlanteans, and they moved with grace and serenity. A gentle melody accompanied everyone, and seemed to echo from every living thing. Sarah and Alyssia were staring in amazement at the iridescent flowers and trees swaying gently in a refreshing breeze, and all the rocks and crystals sparkled dreamily. It was all they could do to concentrate on what was happening around them.

"I feel really tired," exclaimed Alyssia.

Sarah nodded in agreement.

"You will feel tired at first, my friends," explained Eilara, "but you can rest shortly. Everyone who comes here needs an initial rest. But meet my friends first!"

Sarah and Alyssia shook hands with several of the people, who were all women. It was not easy to see which race they were, African, Asian, European, etc., and almost looked like all of them entirely.

"So glad to meet you, Sarah and Alyssia, we don't get many visitors from your kingdom," said one, "my name is Kundara, and I shall show you where you can rest, you can meet everyone else later and we can talk further. I think you really need your rest now!"

Alyssia and Sarah were beginning to get bleary eyed, and were straining to concentrate; despite talking and smiling happily with everyone they met.

"Thank you, it's so beautiful here," remarked Sarah.

"I'd love to draw some of the views!" said Alyssia.

Kundara looked at Alyssia, "I know you would, and it would be wonderful, but we cannot allow you to take any images above ground as yet, for now."

Kundara gave a knowing look, and Alyssia understood, that some things must remain sacred and secret until all is rightly aligned and safe to reveal.

Once inside one of the huts, they found two beds, like springy structures hovering over the floor, with a bed of amethyst and plain quartz crystals underneath.
"Ah! It's like Atlantis!" exclaimed Alyssia.
"Correction is due," said Kundara, "Atlantis was inspired by us!" and they all laughed.
Kundara left with a cheerful wave, and Alyssia and Sarah lay down and were soon asleep.

They awoke gradually, feeling the pleasant energy from the crystals below their beds, as they studied the nature of the room.
"It looks as if it's all made of wood and rushes," remarked Sarah.
"Yes, it's beautiful, and look at that detail over there by the shelf," replied Alyssia.
Sarah spied what Alyssia had seen. It was an unusual lozenge shaped patterned structure on the wall, adjacent to the shelf.
"That looks intriguing," said Sarah, "I'll investigate it later, when I think I can get up!" and she laughed.
"I know!" echoed Alyssia, "I feel so restful, it's hard to move."
"It must be like that change of air syndrome people can get, except it's really exceptionally pure here, the atmosphere that our bodies really need, and takes quite a while to adjust to," explained Alyssia.
"I'll go with that!" agreed Sarah.
There was a knock on their door. It was Kundara.
"Good morning! Kundara here! Would you like to join us for something to eat?"
"Thank you, yes we would," replied Sarah.
"We'll be in the large hall opposite, come when you are ready, ladies," she replied.
They both thanked Kundara and proceeded to stir.
"My goodness, I still feel really tired," exclaimed Sarah.
"Me too!" replied Alyssia, "I hope we can return here for a siesta now and again!" Sarah laughed in response.
They dressed and washed, and proceeded to wander over to the main hall. They looked around at the amazing iridescent golden flowers and trees, as they passed them by, which emanated gentle melodies all the while. Eilara and Kundara greeted them at the door to the main hall, and showed them to their seats.
Sarah and Alyssia looked around, and then at each other with a questioning look.
"What is there to eat?" stated Sarah.

For the tables were empty, save for some sparkling golden hued ornaments down the centre of the tables. One or two of the local inhabitants looked over to the puzzled pair with an understanding smile.

"I'm sure something will be on the cards!" replied Alyssia.

Everyone became silent, with an air of expectancy, and deep peace exuded around everyone and everything. Two dishes of some kind of food appeared above the table they were sitting beside, and gently landed in front of Alyssia and Sarah, much to their surprise, closely followed by two cups of tea.

While Alyssia and Sarah were recovering from their initial surprise, a crowd of drinking vessels appeared, and floated down to their table, in front of everyone, and then also onto the other tables. Sarah examined the drinking vessels to view their contents.

"They look to be holding some kind of fizzy liquid!" exclaimed Sarah, looking to an adjacent person beside her.

"Yes! This is all we need to nourish ourselves here, it holds all the mineral wealth necessary, and rejuvenates and invigorates. You may find, once you are more acclimatised, that you can just be sustained by this, and not need to eat and drink the food you are used to."

"Where does this food and drink of ours come from?" asked Alyssia, "and also your drink?"

"It is asked for from the Divine energy, and is customary here, and is in some parts of your domain. It could become part of many peoples' lives if they wished for it," the person replied, "I should introduce myself, my name is Alandana."

Sarah and Alyssia introduced themselves in response.

"How! You mean you just ask?" enquired Sarah.

"Yes, but the intent must be very pure," said Alandana, pausing for thought to find the right words, "and there is a sense of total altruism to life, and how you live it, for the good of all. If people just wish for it and have any veins of selfishness, it won't come."

Later, Kundara, with Alyssia and Sarah, went into her dwelling place, accompanied by two of her friends. It looked to be twice the size of Alyssia and Sarah's dwelling, made of the same materials. Kundara ushered them to sit down, and she looked around at her friends briefly.

"Now! I can introduce you two to Alyssia and Sarah."

Kundara indicated to her right, and to a slightly taller woman.

"This is one of my co-helpers, and she does a great deal for me, assisting me when I wish to contact the beings who aid Gaia, the Mother spirit of our planet, amongst the many jobs we do together. We ask them what we need to do to help keep things right on the planet, to maintain balance," explained Kundara.

"Hello, my name is Raodhina," she said, and her eyes looked like the centres of flowers, a ring of bright yellow around the iris's, with radiating stripes of orange and red emanating from them. Her skin was a golden colour, with a satin sheen to it, "I'm glad to meet you both."

The other woman came closer and stood beside Alyssia and Sarah, for she had been called to work on a particular job, and had been linked telepathically to a recipient, once Kundara and Raodhina were talking. She was a contrast indeed, for her eyes were like deep wells of turquoise blue, edged in deep royal, and her skin was like Mediterranean waters near any coastline, a paler blue-green shade.

"Hello Sarah and Alyssia, my name is Mimirmaré, and yes, I am linked to Mimir, the being who watches over the subterranean waterways of the world."

"So does Raodhina link to the fire beings, and you, Mimirmaré to the water beings," asked Sarah. "Who links to the Earth, air and ether beings?"

"That is a good question, and one that deserves an answer," said Mimirmaré with a smile, "Kundara is of the ether, and there are two others who are occupied with jobs at present, who assume the roles for Earth and air. Sanjaré is for the Earth, and Zephira is for the air. You may see them, but if not, you will another time. However, we can assume each other's roles if necessary."

Mimirmaré smiled, and her eyes began to turn green and gradually changed to yellow and orange, and her skin went golden. Simultaneously, Raodhina's eyes became turquoise-blue, and her golden skin became a greenish shade, and gradually took on an increasingly deeper turquoise shade. Then they gradually resumed their own colouring again. Then Sarah and Alyssia stopped watching them both avidly.

"You certainly know how the chameleon manages to operate!" exclaimed Alyssia.

"Come! We wish to show you something interesting!" exclaimed Kundara, and the group of them briskly wandered out of the village settlement, that shimmered with a translucent light, like peering through strong sunlight all the time.

Kundara took the lead, while Mimirmaré held onto Sarah, and Raodhina held Alyssia. They all lifted upwards, and hovered six foot above ground, and then they sped off towards an even more dazzling region.

Alyssia and Sarah could perceive a crystalline glow that sparkled. Somehow, they just knew it was a huge crystal, even though no one had mentioned as such, and they were barely able to look at it because it shone so brightly.

"Come over and see if you can touch the crystal," instructed Kundara, "approach gradually my friends, for it has great power."

They approached steadily. Alyssia and Sarah shielded their eyes, and so the others still had to gently lead them closer, until they were in close proximity.

"I still cannot look properly," said Alyssia, half whispering.

"Nor I," agreed Sarah.

Alyssia's hand gradually moved forwards, reaching towards the crystal. She gently touched it and pulled back suddenly.

"Oh! It's like an electric current, and I was seeing connecting lines!" she exclaimed quietly.

Raodhina's hand reached for Alyssia's, and gently replaced it on the crystal, holding it there with her own hand for a moment, as if to stabilise her reaction. Alyssia turned her head, the other hand still shielding her eyes, and smiled towards Raodhina.

Sarah had also reached out and found the energy of the crystal too intense at close quarters, and Mimirmaré had to also hold her hand in hers, and gently replace it onto the crystal.

After a few minutes, Sarah and Alyssia withdrew their hands from the crystal and looked at the others with an inspired expression in their eyes.

"Go on! Tell us what you experienced!" exclaimed Kundara, smiling cheerfully, as were Raodhina and Mimirmaré.

"I could see those connecting lines, linking all the crystals of the world together to the great crystal, and they were lines of bright light, and the healing energy that passed through those lines was in constant flow," explained Alyssia, "and I felt as if all the crystals were in total contact with one another, and I became part of that, and I could see lots of them; some crystals were under the Earth, others in shops, and yet more in the hands of healers, all of them were communicating to one another constantly.

"That's how it is, my friend," confirmed Kundara, "you've seen it truly."

She put her hand on Alyssia's shoulder, and they turned to look at Sarah as she began to speak.

"It was like you felt, Alyssia," began Sarah, "that bolt out of the blue experience of intensity, and it was very powerful, yet it only lasted for less than a few seconds! After that I could see white lines running up through rock fissures and vein lines, giving rock

strata's good energy. This went up to energy sites around the world, Ayers Rock, Stonehenge, and all of those well-known places, as well as mountains with a quantity of igneous rock in them. The thing was, that I could feel the energy going through me too, going towards these places. It must be because we've been touching the crystal, and so we are linked to the network."
"Absolutely true, my friend," agreed Kundara, "couldn't have been explained better."
"Are all places covered adequately by this crystal, or does anywhere need more energy reserves at ground level?" asked Sarah.
"The crystal manages very well, but the nature spirits that work above ground do create their own reserves, given by the crystal and Mother Gaia, the spirit of the planet," explained Kundara.
"Will we be able to see Mother Gaia?" asked Alyssia.
"No reason why not!" said Mimirmaré, "is there, Kundara?"
Kundara listened momentarily elsewhere, her eyes looking afar, and then concentrated upon everyone around her once more.
"Yes, it is fine, we can see her now!" exclaimed Kundara.
They wandered off together, floating away over the top of the greater crystal, and there she was. Strangely, Alyssia and Sarah seemed to instantly know it was Gaia herself.
Mother Gaia smiled, her face assumed that demeanour of an old lady with a shawl over her head. Her eyes shone with an inner light, and the garments she wore around her were all dark brown. She hovered above the crystal's height, in a sitting position, and then floated over to crystal, hovering over it. The others returned to the crystal, and hovered alongside Gaia.
"Welcome!" she said, almost in a whisper, but it came telepathically and everyone heard. She looked kindly towards Alyssia and Sarah, and gave a look of concentration, and then opened her arms out towards them lovingly.
Sarah and Alyssia knew to put out their arms in the same gesture in return, their faces full of joy. Then the group returned to the village.
"You will know the full meaning of the visit to Mother Gaia soon, my friends," said Kundara.
"We could feel what she meant, she was so powerfully still, like she wanted us to be as strong too," explained Alyssia.
"Yes, and to know what she wants to happen on Earth, from her perspective," commented Sarah, "I mean, we knew about environmental concerns and resourceful living before, but somehow, through this meeting, the understanding is much more profound."
Kundara, Raodhina and Mimirmaré smiled and nodded.

Alyssia and Sarah returned to their smaller dwelling to take stock of the meeting, and they talked together for a while. When the conversation had run its course, Sarah looked over to that lozenge shaped artefact by the shelf.

"We never found out what that thing is, did we?" she said, going over to the lozenge and examining it. "It just looks like a decoration, Alyssia."

"Well, that sounds nice, I suppose," commented Alyssia, "try touching it and see what happens!" she added, with a grin.

Sarah pressed it, and a shower of gold and silver sparks came out. She gave an involuntary cry of surprise, and then they both laughed. Sarah returned to her bed and lay down. The gold and silver sparks, which had appeared suddenly, and fizzled away equally swiftly. They then reappeared slowly, and began to glide around the room, and permeated the whole of the dwelling, wrapping them up in an aura of peaceful and restorative energy.

"Well! It's an energy source and wonderful!" said Sarah, thoughtfully.

"I think it's linked to the crystals under the bed now," commented Alyssia, "can you feel it; the energy is getting stronger!"

"It certainly is! We might take off!" rejoined Sarah.

There was a knock at the door, and Kundara peeped round it.

"It is time for you to return above ground, my friends," said Kundara, "once the Source energy is discovered, we know you will know all that's necessary here!" she beckoned them.

Alyssia and Sarah floated from their beds and out of the door, much to their surprise.

There was Eilara, waiting for them. Alyssia and Sarah exchanged goodbyes with Kundara, Mimirmaré and Raodhina. Two figures were becoming visible in the distance, Sanjaré and Zephira! Then they were beside them! Alyssia and Sarah could feel the pristine love and harmony of this place more and more intensely.

Eilara led them back upwards. They waved to the others, but knew there were no goodbyes, as they felt so connected to everyone there. Once inside the tunnels, Eilara left them, and Alyssia and Sarah just seemed to fly up them with ease, until they landed in the centre of the crystal circle once more. Alyssia reached inside a purse she had attached to her belt, inside it lay her Glorae-astraesphere. She picked it up, holding it in the palm of her hand. She imagined it was a tiny Astragandara floating in space. It rose gently from her palm, and an

astonished Alyssia looked at Sarah. Sarah got out her Gloraeastraesphere, and soon she was doing the same.
"Levitation was mentioned by Galaron!" said Sarah.
They put the crystals away, picked up the last remnants of food lying on their rugs and walked out of the circle, touching the nearest crystals gratefully. The rugs disappeared, and they set off down the mountainside, half walking, and half hovering all the way down.

"I think we've found what we were looking for, as much as we can perceive for now," explained Sarah.
"Yes, I think so too. It's been successful," added Alyssia.
"I'm so glad," responded Galaron, "I certainly feel you've both learnt quite a lot in a short time."
"I suppose we can't stay any longer, or we won't wish to return to our time period!" said Alyssia.
"No, off you go before you take root!" said Galaron, and he laughed jovially.
They gave each other hugs, and then stood looking at one another.
"Do you think you are ready to travel to the future?" asked Galaron.
"Will it be different to going back into the past?" asked Sarah.
"It can be, though it is always best to go much further than in your own life time, of course," advised Galaron, "you'll be fine."

Then Alyssia and Sarah brought out their crystals, and concentrated on Sarah's well, once more.

Chapter 4 – Preparing the Ground

"So, you can levitate now!" exclaimed Kenny, jovially, "will you give Karin and I a demonstration!" and he winked.
Sarah and Alyssia smiled in response.
"Sorry to disappoint you, but only when necessary, as it uses up a lot of energy," explained Alyssia.
"Fair enough," responded Kenny, "why lift something with your mind power, if an arm can do it much easier. He added, with a thoughtful expression, "If it happens naturally, without effort, then I can see that it's okay, like some of the saints in olden times I've read about who would find themselves being lifted into the air."
"Is it alright to see the Glorae-astraespheres?" asked Karin.
"We have brought them," said Sarah.
Alyssia and she rummaged around in their bags, and then carefully placed them on their velveteen pouches, on the kitchen table. Kenny and Karin leaned forwards and examined the crystals closely. After a period of silence, Kenny, looking visibly moved, began to speak.
"The name fits them! I can't find the words, and mainly just felt profoundly moved by them, as if they were beckoning me homeward, though not sure I've come from Astragandara, like you two!" exclaimed Kenny.
"I felt the same as Kenny," ventured Karin, "somehow I was aware of a beautiful melody that was so sweet and gentle, that I couldn't help being profoundly moved myself."
Karin stopped speaking, and began to form tears in her eyes.
Kenny nodded, "That's something I heard too, but couldn't speak about it," and he also began to look almost moved to tears.
"We know, it's very moving," sympathised Sarah, "I think so much was going on, we didn't have time to ponder on it, besides, we were surrounded by angelic beings from the planet, which helped, when we meditated together."
"I wonder when you will understand about Gaia?" asked Kenny in almost a whisper.
"We think that is the main thing, the most important aspect of it all," said Alyssia.
"Not sure when, maybe it needs meditating on," said Sarah.
"Perhaps we can all meditate on it, and see what happens," suggested Alyssia.
They all reached their hands across the table, and joined as one together over the Glorae-astraespheres. Sarah and Alyssia then arose; while Kenny said he'd better get back to the shop.

"We'll get back to Ty Craig then, and see what comes over the next few days, eh folks!" said Sarah.

"We'll call you if we get anything," said Karin, "back to duties in the office."

They all hugged each other, and Kenny led the way downstairs, and he took the door into the shop from the stairwell, and the other two took the outer door to the small car parking area at the back, and then drove back to Sarah's home.

One morning, a day or two after their meeting, Sarah had just finished an early breakfast, and was wandering around the garden to check her vegetables. Alyssia was meditating in her room upstairs. Sunlight gleamed through an overcast sky, and that light cast a strong profile over Sarah's face, and her eyes narrowed as a result. Upstairs, Alyssia could feel the warming rays on her as she focused her mind, thinking of Gaia.

A glowing image of the shawled figure came to mind again, and with the outstretched arms. 'I feel we must all know her, really know the Earth, and be in contact with her, and all of life at the deepest levels possible,' Alyssia thought.

"I suppose we shall know what that entails as we progress," said Sarah to Alyssia, when Alyssia had told her about the meditation.

"Yes, it is only a start, I know," said Alyssia, and she stopped speaking. She looked over to when Sarah had begun to concentrate on, up in the clouds.

"Sorry to interrupt you, but look at those clouds, there are two identical ones, one dark and the other light, and on opposite coloured backgrounds," explained Sarah.

"Yes, yin and yang clouds," responded Alyssia, "it's like the intrinsic nature of the one is in the other, and also links the realms of Heaven and Earth together, and the working out of cycles and a sense of completion. Once that is done, once all that is needed to be expressed at a particular level is completed, then life moves on to the next, and so on, until there is no need for physical life as we know it. Not sure when all that will be completed, I'm sure. However, regarding what is relevant to Gaia, we must meditate upon her and see what else will come to mind."

"I don't think I can add to that at present! I have been aware of a presence somehow, like as if we are being watched benignly. Perhaps it is by Gaia herself!" responded Sarah.

That afternoon saw Alyssia working on the trilogy once more, while Sarah was baking. Sarah put a cake, some biscuits and a savoury pie into the oven and washed up.
"How's the story progressing?" called out Sarah.
"Doing well, I have written up a lot of it in full, as far as Anchorin's visit to the Garden of Eden," said Alyssia; "you're welcome to read it over any time."
"I will!" replied Sarah, "Oh look! It's sunny outside!"
"Good!" exclaimed Alyssia, "do you mind if I go out and so some sketching, as I'd like to do a painting of the well."
"That's fine," responded Sarah, "I'll be editor!"

There was a knock at the back door a while later, when Alyssia had finished her sketches of the well, and she had also done a view of the hillfort of Pen Craig. Sarah went to see who was there.
"Hello Hudlath, nice to see you! Do come in!" exclaimed Sarah.
"Don't mind if I do!" responded Hudlath emphatically, and he smiled.
They went through to the lounge, and Sarah called up to Alyssia, who ran swiftly downstairs, to join them.
"I've come to give you all the final two sets of the chakra cards," said Hudlath, "here! A set for each of you two, and copies for Kenny and Karin."
"What will happen after we've finished doing these cards, Hudlath?" asked Alyssia.
"We might even be as wise as Hudlath and Anchorin!" quipped Sarah, and they all burst out laughing.
"There could be a grain of truth in that remark, joking aside!" remarked Hudlath, with a mischievous look, "however, seriously, they link you to the universal energy, and prepare you for finer energy sources, for a specific reason," and he looked meaningfully at both Alyssia and Sarah.
"Could you tell us this specific reason, or even give us a hint of what it entails?" asked Sarah.
"Well, it will come clear after you've done the cards, my friends. You will be called by Anchorin, let me admit to that!" said Hudlath, smiling slightly, "sorry to seem enigmatic!"
Sarah and Alyssia looked at each other, resignedly, and said "Ok! We'll just have to be patient, I suppose."
As it was late, Hudlath declined a cup of tea, saying he had to return and initiate a training session with his priests.

"I keep wondering about this secrecy, Alyssia," remarked Sarah.

"Yes, I know that we have to experience things for ourselves, but, the mystery factor seems overdone to me. Oh well, we'll see where all this mystery takes us eventually, no doubt," added Alyssia.
"This is the weekend we decided to meet up and go around the sites, to link them to the starway system again," remarked Sarah.
"Oh right!" responded Alyssia, "I'll text the others and remind them, and tell them about the cards."
"We can all have a card session then too. See if Sunday suits them," said Sarah.
Alyssia sent the text, and then they went upstairs to their bedrooms.

A pair of emerald eyes shone with an inner light. A pathway linked through them both, into a sea of emerald through a gate, and then over a circular pond. There was a dazzling burst of light and Alyssia could see Melendra's face. She was the being from the village of huts in the next realm Alyssia and Sarah had meditated on.
"Where am I?" she asked.
"A place you haven't been to before, but the High Priest of Atlantis has!" replied Melendra.
Alyssia awoke, wondering what it meant.

"Over a circular pond?" questioned Sarah, over breakfast, "is there anything else you saw in the dream we can identify with?"
"I went through a gate into a very beautiful part of nature, and Melendra said the High Priest of Atlantis had been there, either Anchorin or Hudlath," pondered Alyssia.
They both stopped in thought for a moment.
"It's Anchorin!" exclaimed Alyssia.
"Then it could be the Garden of Eden!" cried Sarah.
"Then maybe we will have to visit it," said Alyssia.
"Maybe, once we've completed the last two sets, Alyssia," concluded Sarah.
"That painting of the well looks intriguing, Alyssia!"
Sarah peered interestedly at the image a moment, for Alyssia had depicted the well with some of the codes incised around its bowl, and energy arising out of it, and around the whole area as well.
The morning was bright, catching the far side of the trees by the well, illumining their outer edges, and alighting on the foliage all around.

"They should be here in a few minutes!" cried Sarah, having looked at her watch.
"We'd better get a move on!" responded Alyssia, "I'll just get myself some lunch ready before they come!"

"Hop in, folks!" exclaimed Kenny cheerfully, as Sarah and Alyssia came out of the cottage, with their backpacks, and got into the car.
"Hi! Where is it we're going again?" asked Karin.
"Woolston well, it's east of the A483," explained Sarah, "and it's west of West Felton."
"Oh yes, I seem to remember us going to West Felton one day when we were exploring the area on our arrival, and had a nice meal in a restaurant there," said Kenny.
"I remember the day, that meal came after a lot of driving around the perimeter of Oswestry," responded Karin.
"Well, I know it's not far away, but we were tired after setting up the shop," explained Kenny, "and we thought we would have a look out for interesting ancient sites, and I'd say to Karin, anything interesting here, while I was concentrating on driving, and there would invariably be no reply as she'd fallen asleep. After doing that for a while, we ended up at West Felton at about eight o'clock, with me determined we get something to eat, after failing to explore efficiently!"
"That's not fair!" replied Karin, laughing, "we did find a few good places even if I did close my eyes on occasions."
"We believe you!" cried Alyssia and Sarah, and Kenny turned his head and winked at them.
They approached a T-junction, and Karin said to turn left, and Kenny accelerated off onto a wider road.
"There's a fort to our right, which we will visit later on," said Sarah, "after the well, and the next one is the fort at Criggion."
"We can either take the short route or the longer, more countrified route," said Karin, as Kenny approached a small crossroads, "short to the left, and …"
Before Karin could finish the sentence, Kenny had veered left, and moved swiftly to Woolston.
"I don't recall you driving as fast before you met Jadeir," remarked Karin.
Kenny laughed, "You could be right there, dear. I'd better try to become a bit more sedate!"

They came into the little hamlet, looked over to where the river was, and began walking down there. Once by the well, which was a very small aperture amongst thick undergrowth, with a tiny streamlet running to the river Morda, they began their ceremony.

"Let us cast a circle of light around us," said Sarah, and she drew her wand around all of them, walking around the circle, "and bring in good energy, and linking to Heaven and Earth. Let us now link to the starway junction of meeting points, drawing upon the three intersecting circles' energy of the universe, to bring down into the site here."

Everyone had their wands pointing to the starway, and they focused on linking to that energy, ready to bring it down.

"Let us now bring that energy into the circle of light, that it may enter this well," said Sarah, and she drew down her wand, and pointed it towards the well, and everyone else did also, visualising the energy going in. There was a stirring of bright energy, and the light began to pour in.

Afterwards, they walked back to the car, eager to reach the next place.

"I could see those intersecting circles associated with water, coming down into the well area," commented Alyssia.

"How lovely!" responded Karin, "it just felt good to me! Oh! Next stop Criggion, Kenny!" she exclaimed.

They sped further down the A483, and then turned onto a B road that led to Shrewsbury.

"We continue to Crew Green, where the road leads upto behind the fort," explained Sarah, "as the path will save us a lot of climbing from there!"

"Good thinking, Sarah!" cried Karin, "oh yes, I see the route!"

"It looks very coniferous, I hope we don't get lost in there," said Kenny.

"There are actually quite a lot of paths, it's a well-known area, I'd say, dear," responded Karin.

Once in the forestry track ways, they followed a main footpath that crossed another track way, and continued onwards, and then diverted to the left, up to the top of the fort. Once they felt they were in the right area, they began the ceremony, as before, but Alyssia took charge this time. When they all felt the energy was good and strong, they returned to the car, and were back up the A483 to Llanymynech. The fort was on the hill to the west side of the main road, just south of Llynclys. After their session, they found a favourable place and sat to eat some lunch.

"Can you feel a sense of linking up with the sites now?" asked Alyssia, "it feels to me that a circuit is being born."

The others murmured in agreement, lost in thought for now.

They then went to St Oswald's Well, parking up a nearby street, and walked to the well that had a wall built around it. They conducted the ceremony as best as they could in a fairly public place, but still managed to see the good energy coming in from the starway junction.

"Castle Mound! That brings back a few memories!" stated Kenny.
They were back in the car again, moving northwards out of Oswestry. Once at a junction point, Kenny hesitated, giving Karin a questioning look.
"Turn right here, and then next left for the footpath," responded Karin.
Kenny duly took the first turn off, and continued to the next junction, and they found a parking area off that minor road.
"Ha! I recognise this now!" exclaimed Kenny, "on familiar territory!"
They clambered out of the car, and walked along the tiny road, and soon found an entrance across the fields to the mound.
"There's certainly a lot more water than the last time we were here, look!" exclaimed Alyssia, "it's almost into this wood, and it must be almost a circle!"
"A bit like your dream, Alyssia," remarked Sarah.
"Yes, indeed!" exclaimed Alyssia, and she explained it to Karin and Kenny.
"There could be a link here that's relevant," said Kenny.
With that, they reached the castle mound, and a burst of sunlight momentarily created a dazzling mirror of the pond's water.
"An impressive sight!" said Sarah, and then she cast the circle, and they distributed the light into the Earth. As the light revealed itself to everyone, a face appeared to them, with intense green eyes.
"We of the elemental kingdoms are pleased at your work, and wish you to know it will be very helpful to nature," he said, "and I have a guest who wishes to be made known to you!" said the elf, who had finally shown himself fully.
There was a shimmer of green light, and a familiar figure emerged.
"Jadeir!" everyone cried.
"It's about time I visited you all!" he exclaimed, smiling broadly, "where's that boyo?" and he looked at Kenny and gave him a slap on the shoulder, and Kenny returned him one.

The two elves shook hands, and then the visitor elf disappeared, before the group all headed back to the car.
"How have you all been since I've been away?" asked Jadeir.
"It seems like we are slowly building up to another mission, Jadeir," explained Sarah, "Alyssia and I have been back in time recently to Lemuria to a crystal circle, and before that we visited the spirit worlds."
"We also visited the centre of the Earth," added Alyssia, "and we strongly feel that there is something relevant to be learned from our meetings with Gaia."
"Our dear Mother Gaia," remarked Jadeir, and his eyes became clear and translucent, and gradually filled with a soft velvety light, "I shall meditate on Gaia for you."
They were now back in the car and off to the next site.
"We'll go northwards, Kenny, and miss the Oswestry traffic," said Karin.
"Don't mind if I do, dear!" responded Kenny.
They repeated the ceremony once more up at Oswestry hill fort, where they first went to Atlantis, and then they returned to the shop car park.
"You know I've invited you to a meal at my place!" said Sarah.
"I just need to get something!" exclaimed Kenny, and he ran off. Jadeir leapt from the car and followed him, and they raced each other to the back door, and went inside.
"A couple of kids, they are!" laughed Karin.

"Now! What do you want to tell me, Jadeir?" asked Kenny, earnestly, his shock of curly hair added to the intensity of his expression, and lost his usual comical appearance, temporarily.
"Gaia wishes you to know something very deep, and very earnest, my friend," explained Jadeir.
"What is it?" asked Kenny; "I know Alyssia and Sarah are trying to find out, after seeing her in Agartha."
"Yes, but we elementals are in touch the most effectively, because of our natures," explained Jadeir, "anyway, the truth is that we must keep our minds linked constantly with all that is beneficent. Forget listening to the news, and all Earthly problems, just concentrate on what you can do! There is much more you can all do, but you cannot see it yet, can you?"
"Like what?" asked Kenny, wondering why Jadeir was like this, after all, he and Karin were keeping the shop running, which provided a service promoting spirituality, and Alyssia sold her paintings. Now they were getting the story of their journeys to Atlantis written, which they thought would be of interest.

"There is much more you could do, but you have to find out for yourself. Ask Gaia what she needs, and what else you have to offer," persisted Jadeir, emphatically. Kenny still looked quite oddly at Jadeir. "I know Gaia wants something more from your group, and Gaia urged me to tell you," continued Jadeir, "you know you all have a lot to offer, and there is more potential there. Just ponder on it and see!"
"I'll give it a whirl then, okay?" said Kenny, "now I'd better reappear outside, with the thing I was supposed to be coming inside for!"
"How about these?" asked Jadeir, reaching for some biscuits.
"Good choice! Karin's best buy!" responded Kenny.
They both returned to the car speedily.

"Let's go!" exclaimed Kenny, and he drove off down to Sarah's home once more.
Once inside her cottage, Sarah mentioned about the cards, and handed packs to Karin and Kenny.
"If you'll be card working, I'll just go and have a look around your garden, and have a talk with the local folk," said Jadeir, "I know about your two famous well friends, Alendrin and Miara."
"Oh!" exclaimed Sarah, "so you've met them already?"
"Indeed! We had a nice chat, for I can talk to any beings, instantly, both within the area and at a distance!" replied Jadeir.
"You're welcome, Jadeir, just come and go as you please. I shall be putting out some cake shortly!" replied Sarah.
Jadeir looked interested, and then went outdoors.
"Do you feel ready to do the cards yet, folks? I suspect a cuppa will be welcomed first!" asked Sarah.
"Yes, great!" was the general response.
Jadeir, meanwhile, went straight to the well and began speaking to Alendrin and Miara.
"Do you think they know much of what they are intending to do in this life? What Gaia is hoping for?" asked Jadeir.
"They are trying their best, and always responding to what appears to be guiding them, but, like most humans, however wonderfully kind and devoted they are, find it very hard to know the full gamut of what is possible," responded Alendrin.
"We always wish more people could intuit and see what is really required, for there are inner truths and realms to be found, which could bring so many resources into view. Things that would give new purposes to many," said Miara.
"I know indeed, as you describe it now," responded Jadeir, us Atlanteans know how it is in a Golden Age, and also that in our time, the general public are quite simplistic, but happy to look

upto the priesthood for their every direction in life, unlike this age now, where people are on the verge of self-emancipation of a bigger scale, yet don't have all the tools to hand, even though there are some of those resources around, because they either cannot reach, or don't understand, yet. Yes, there are diverse levels of people here, from devoted and spiritual, those who are good and conscientious who may not be oriented to spirituality, to a fair few who steal and harm others."

"Sarah and Alyssia, Karin and Kenny, will have to understand the next phase of their lives. It will happen once they meditate on Gaia, and finish the sets of cards. At least I genuinely hope so!" explained Miara.

The other two also shared the same opinion.

"I hear the kettle going, and crockery being moved about!" said Jadeir, and he flashed a quick smile, and went indoors again.

"Let's have a look at these cards," said Kenny, and he handed the other pack to Karin.

"Intergalactic Lore, and Linking to Eternity," commented Karin, "it sounds interesting!"

"Yes, I'm looking forward to it!" responded Alyssia.

"What will you do Jadeir, while we do these cards?" asked Sarah, "there's a lovely hillfort nearby, if you want to explore."

"I had thought you lot had already started on those cards!" exclaimed Jadeir, "I bet Kenny held things up, asking for biscuits!"

"Now, behave yourself boyo!" responded Kenny with a penetrating look, "or no cake for you!" and Jadeir laughed heartily.

"Okay folks, I shall visit the hillfort, after another chat by the well, and then go over to Pistyll Rhaeadr and see my friends there, bye folks!" explained Jadeir. Everyone waved to him in response as he left through the back door.

The attention veered towards the cake and a cup of herbal tea for the required time period.

The only distraction was that one piece of cake lifted itself up and levitated outside through the back door.

"That Jadeir never misses a trick!" exclaimed Kenny.

The group focused on the first pack, Linking to Intergalactic Lore.

"Right everyone, crown chakra, right brained image," announced Sarah, "shall we aim for about ten minutes, and then compare notes?"

"That should be fine, Sarah," said Alyssia, "if anyone needs more time, we can just wait."

They all agreed on that, and made a start. They each brought the card upto the third eye, focused on it a moment, and then closed their eyes and continued to hold the card in place. Once everyone's eyes opened again, Sarah indicated for Kenny to start.

"I was aware of a strong solar power, like with the three intersecting ovals," he said.

"I was aware of strong energy coming downwards too, and almost a smell of frankincense and rose combined," said Karin.

"I also felt strong energy coming and it was vibrant," said Alyssia.

"I also felt the strong energy, and it emanated from my hands and feet," agreed Sarah. "Now, we must do this for the emotional, mental and spiritual levels."

They found the same principle of strong energy flow at all levels, but more gentle with the emotional, and more intense with the mental, and encompassing for the spiritual level, throughout the outer layers of the auric space.

They launched into the crown chakra, left brained image, focusing on it for a while, and then reconvened for discussion.

"I felt that strong energy at work again, and coming out of my soles," commented Kenny.

"I could see an image of four columns of light radiating energy to me," said Karin.

"I saw those four columns too, and a fiery circle with a heart inside it, and then it turned into a six pointed star that was between the four columns," said Alyssia.

"I felt that the energy of the Universe was coming through me," concluded Sarah.

The same effects came via the other layers, but all a bit more strongly, as the left brained images are the ones that manifest the energy that is brought in by the right brained ones.

The group went through the third eye cards also, and then found enough energy to do the throat chakra cards as well.

Jadeir's head popped around the lounge door, just then.

"Greetings all! How was your session? I'd like to know what results you got."

They described the crown chakra cards, and then began on the third eye ones.

"I think, to sum up the third eye cards, they had a scouring action on the third eye, to ensure the eye was pure and whole to receive good wisdom at all levels, etheric, emotional, mental and spiritual. It also scoured the other head chakras too, and also

someone got the phrase 'my head is in the stars and my feet are on the Earth.' That more or less sums it up," concluded Sarah.
"What about the throat cards, but that sounds right so far for the crown and third eye," said Jadeir, putting his hand on Kenny's shoulder.
"The energy was gentle here, initially, lifting emotional levels so that Heaven and Earth met, in order to consolidate this. At the mental level the energy was stronger, as expected, and then the left brained cards brought in stronger columns of energy, zapping the throat area, and out through the feet very strongly. Some very high energy coming in here," concluded Sarah, again.
Jadeir nodded approvingly.
"You are beginning to see the dawn of something wonderful here. Keep it coming," he said, encouragingly.

Over the next few days, the four of them concentrated on completing the Intergalactic Lore, and the Linking to Eternity sets of cards. Meanwhile, Jadeir went over to see the nature spirits he met at Pistyll Rhaeadr again, and met them when he first visited the Oswestry group before their rescue mission to Colony Y. He returned to Sarah's cottage when he knew that the group had finished.

"You know, that strong energy that has been tuning us to the Infinite is definitely working!" exclaimed Alyssia.
"Yes, my head and feet are glowing, indeed!" agreed Sarah.
They were sitting just outside the backdoor at Sarah's cottage, having eaten their breakfast. The morning light shone sharply through the trees on the Craig fort, to their east, so that Sarah and Alyssia's view showed sunlight coming upon the well, and the trees around it, the top of the apple trees to the right and the grass beside them. Sarah and Alyssia were in the shade, but it was a very warm day, so it didn't matter. Alyssia and Sarah looked meaningfully at each other.
"It's a strange feeling I've got," commented Alyssia, "I feel kind of restless, as if expecting something to happen."
"You took the words right out of my mouth," smiled Sarah.
A greenish light appeared at the well, and then a pair of green eyes became visible.
"Those look like Jadeir's eyes!" exclaimed Alyssia.
Jadeir appeared, smiling, and leapt out of the well.
"Good morning to you two!" he exclaimed, cheerfully, "I've been to see Kenny and Karin, and asked them to come over, we're all going to Atlantis!"

"But who will look after the shop?" asked Sarah.
"Don't worry! We'll return at the same time we left, this time!" replied Jadeir, "or near enough, besides, it is a Sunday!"
"Let's get prepared!" said Alyssia, getting up swiftly. They took their chairs indoors, and gathered essentials together for their journey.

Meanwhile, a few minutes later, a car came to a halt outside the cottage gate, and Jadeir answered the door a moment later.
"Hello Karin and Kenny, do come in!"
"We'll be down shortly!" cried Sarah from upstairs.

Jadeir eagerly led the four friends across the back garden to Sarah's well by the trees, for the foliage in the garden had thickened out favourably. Alendrin and Miara showed up and cheerfully waved to them all.
"By the blessings of Mimir and all of us, may your journey bear good fruit!" they said.
"Thank you, friends," replied the Oswestry group, simultaneously.
Sarah and the others had already become Atlantean sized, having taken the elixir tincture to reach that size, and were wearing their Atlantean clothing. They all drew out their wands and focused on 12,000 years BC, when Anchorin the high priest of the mountain temple of Atlantis was extant. There was a shimmer of light, and they all disappeared from the twenty first century.

Alendrin and Miara looked at each other.
"Do you think they know what they will be doing?" commented Alendrin.
"No, I don't think so yet, but they will, once they reach their next destination," replied Miara.
Alendrin looked thoughtful a moment.
"Yes, I think they will, indeed!"
They both smiled happily, exuded a sparkling misty energy that radiated out and permeated all the vegetables nearby, which all responded with an inaudible to human ears sense of 'ah!' and then the two elementals vanished from view again.

Chapter 5 – Journey to Eden

Sarah, Alyssia, Karin, Kenny and Jadeir arrived safely at the foot of the mountain. The beautiful waterfall nearby that reminded Sarah of a life as a wise woman was still producing crystalline, sparkling water. The vivid greens of the moss-encrusted rocks glistened in the sunlight were enhanced by the water's spray. Fairies and elves still worked and danced around the waters edge, and undines bobbed up to the water's surface periodically.
"The energy here is still just as phenomenal as ever," exclaimed Alyssia.
"The light shining on those crystals look so lovely too," remarked Sarah.
"It certainly is a splendid healing place," responded Karin.
They all gathered around for a few minutes to savour the atmosphere.
"Ho all!" cried Jadeir, and everyone turned their heads to look at him, with an expression in their faces of people coming out of a reverie. "We'd better get going folks! Sorry to spoil your meditation!"
They all walked around to the track that goes directly up the mountain, and with that intention of theirs to ascend it brought a mountain buggy to their feet. They were soon ascending to the summit.
"My heart always fills with joy on seeing that beautiful temple, with the orichalcum dome," said Karin, her face animated.
"Yes, even though it's often shrouded in mists," echoed Kenny.
Jadeir led the group to the entrance, and spoke to the attendant priest.
Shortly, the tall figure of Anchorin appeared, with his long grey hair, and alert, violet eyes. He smiled at the group, and his eyes took on an electrically charged animation, as the group described it.
"So glad you could all come together, we've been expecting you, follow me!"
He disappeared inside the temple, and everyone had to walk sprightly, to keep up, and they all found themselves in a conference room. The walls were as they expected, carved out of the rock of the mountain, as the whole temple had been.

Anchorin ushered them to seats. They looked in surprise to see Zanadar, Aurion and Salaron, from Cassiopeia, Sirius and the Pleiades, respectively, and from that present time period. They all exchanged greetings, briefly.

"Now!" announced Anchorin, "we have to consider the next task your group has to perform."

Anchorin gestured to Zanadar to begin procedures.

"I wish to say initially, that your work on the sites around Oswestry has begun the anchoring process, as planned. You won't notice much at present, and other people even less, but within a certain amount of time, there will be a definite change that will come about."

Zanadar looked around at everyone in the Oswestry group, to note their reactions, if any. His orange-pink face, typical of Cassiopeians, had a magenta tinge to it, which usually meant he had been travelling in places that were not the most challenging of environments, and so the better energy was showing in a more refined shade, as a result.

"Can I ask what kind of change?" queried Kenny.

"Yes you may," responded Zanadar, "it will ensure that the quality of time and space will begin to be altered."

"How can it be altered?" asked Karin, "and what symptoms will become apparent?"

Zanadar smiled, "I like lots of questions, keep them coming! It will be altered because increasingly stronger energies from higher realms will begin to pour in, and the slower and lower vibrations and preoccupations will begin to find themselves out on a limb, and if some conscientious people are aware of them, they can send them into the light, and be of good help."

"Will any people rebel more than they do at present?" asked Alyssia.

"There will come a time when people like that will either pass over and move to other three dimensional worlds, sadly, or realise that what they are doing is futile, and to offer something useful is the best way forward," replied Zanadar.

He looked around questioningly at the others.

"What is it we are here for now?" asked Sarah and Kenny simultaneously.

"Well! That's the best question!" replied Aurion, and everyone laughed.

"We wish you to visit the Garden of Eden," commented Salaron, "once there, the Sentinel will give you further instructions."

"We can't ask anything more from you about this?" asked Alyssia.

"I'm sorry, but it will have to remain one of those experiential tasks, and because even we don't know everything that is involved," explained Aurion.

"All we can say is that we understand about working here and there around this universe, and sometimes neighbouring ones,

that you need to have a sense of the understanding of time, synchronicity, and whether actions are required or not," explained Zanadar, "because if you don't realise these things in entirety, you could cause yourselves karmic repercussions through an unpremeditated action," advised Aurion.
"But how can you know exactly?" asked Karin, looking as anxious as everyone else was, now.
"There are signs, but you will find out, I know you all will, otherwise you wouldn't be here, about to go on this journey. Be reassured, my friends, we just need to help you realise the full gamut of everything that is entailed in what you will be involved in, that is all!" explained Zanadar.
The anxious look on the group's faces began to fade. Then Anchorin got up, and went to the corner of the room near the door, and held his hand, palm up, near the wall, and a light began to appear. He returned to sit down, for all their chairs were in a semi circle looking towards that wall.
"I have a bit of entertainment for you all to watch!" announced Anchorin, and he smiled with a hint of mischief in his eyes, "not one of your blockbusters, I hasten to add!"

They all focused on the light on the wall, which became increasingly brighter, until the group found it a bit difficult to look at. Then there was a chorus of song, and a sense of travelling at speed.
"Link to us and you will find your way forward!" came a voice to Alyssia's mind. She focused on the voice as strongly as she could. She could feel herself moving into a deep green crystalline structure, and felt as if the energy of it permeated her whole being, and she knew a greater sense of linking with nature. It was a deepening of awareness that linked her with all of life. She found herself unable to recall any more until she awoke again. She looked around at the others, and found that they were awaking also. Alyssia described what she had experienced to everyone.
"Yes, I had that too!" commented Sarah.
"So did I!" was echoed several times.
"So we all experienced the same thing!" exclaimed Kenny.
"Yes you did, because you've all had to begin that extra deep link with nature and life itself," commented Anchorin, "it will help you when you visit the Garden of Eden."
The light on the wall was now a bright rose colour, and the group all began looking at it again.
"Come in, come to the centre…." Sarah heard, and it sounded like words formed on a breeze, or in the rustle of leaves. She

found herself spiralling into the centre of that roseate light, through masses of rose quartz crystals, and she felt the glow of their energy in her heart. It was as if the whole Earth's love was focused through these crystals, saturating her through with it. A mauve light became apparent through this, and it seemed she became immersed in a sea of amethyst crystal. She knew it was the huge crystal at the centre of the Earth, not to be found on the physical level, but the higher astral onwards.
"We have been waiting, waiting for so long!" heard Sarah, "when will you help us fully?"
"What can I do?" asked Sarah, "I am more than happy to do whatever is required."
"Good, you will discover soon!" came the reply.
Sarah drifted off, and then awoke to find out everyone else had experienced exactly the same as her.

Anchorin smiled, and then activated the next stage.
The light on the wall became a green-turquoise shade, and began to pulsate slowly. The colour gradually deepened to a luminous deep sky blue, and a spiral of stars appeared at its centre.
"Inside each star lies all the components of life, the nucleus of the universal life, the galaxy, and the solar system, and your atoms hold my energy, know it, feel it, see it!" heard Karin.
She felt herself being drawn deep inside the central star, and felt its fiery light illumine the source of energy in her mind, and potentise her being. There was a feeling of wallowing and bathing in that light, floating through it in an extremely still atmosphere that no Earthly noise could reach.

Karin drifted off peacefully, and then awoke to find herself looking at the others, and knowing they had experienced this too, and they all smiled at each other knowingly.
"You may think you have topped the whole experience, but there is more!" said Anchorin gently, so as not to disturb their state of reverie.
Zanadar and his compatriots sat peacefully with gentle smiles on their faces.

Anchorin activated the stage to follow, and everyone began to look at the illumined wall, which had shades of green, a pale reddish brown, like a horse chestnut, and a kaleidoscopic selection of other colours fleetingly came through. There was that feeling of moving towards the centre again, followed by a sense of pushing through thick foliage. A rich chorus of birdsong arose, with that intensity of a dawn chorus in springtime, of all kinds of birds, not just from one country. It was from all over the planet, all singing as if with one voice!

Kenny wondered how that could be, when instantly several pairs of green eyes looked at him, and then many brown eyes of many varieties of creatures.

"Hello!" he said in his usual buoyant way, and there was a chorus of yelps, roars, bellows and all varieties of responses, and the green eyes showed the rest of their faces, elven, fey, sylph and undine, and their response came once the animals cries had stopped, and it was likewise a greeting woven into a chorus of melodies.

Kenny felt very moved, and just when the melody reached a crescendo, huge beings of light surrounded him, and he knew they were of the Devic Kingdom, and he could feel their deep strength and overseeing power of nature. Out from behind them, a strong, tall being with deep brown penetrating eyes came forward, and his gentle horns and cloven hooves indicated to Kenny who he was.

"Pan and the Devic Kingdom too, this is an honour!" exclaimed Kenny.

"It is what you will do, that is why we are here!" they said in response.

Kenny's face held a fleeting expression of puzzlement.

"Well, I'm not sure what!" he murmured.

"Worry not, you WILL know, my friend," said Pan, encouragingly.

Kenny smiled peacefully, and the chorus of birds returned a short while, and then he drifted off. When he awoke, there were some more faces looking at him, Karin and the others, and they all shared that they had identical experiences once more.

Anchorin stirred, and the light on the wall faded.

"Well, I think you have all done well, and understood what each message holds," said Anchorin, "and now the only thing to do is to go to Eden!"

The conference concluded with that. Zanadar, Aurion and Salaron said their farewells, and took to the skies. Anchorin provided the group with a meal and then they all made ready to leave the temple.

The mountain buggy was awaiting as the Oswestry group came out of the temple, and they stood a moment to take in some fresh air.

"I shall accompany you a certain way, and then I must leave you to continue," informed Anchorin, having now accompanied them.

They all got into the buggy and descended out of the mountain mist to view the panorama, now being revealed. The bright arcing lights that appeared over trees, showing their auric energies, and electric blue ley lines criss-crossing the land into the distance. The elves and fairies tending trees and flowers with their healing energy, making the plants grow, and the sound of the waterfall at the foot of the mountain, becoming increasingly more audible.
"We will need a hoverbuggy when we reach the base of the mountain, if we can get one soon enough!" cried Anchorin, and he focused hard with intent.

"It is around the other side of those mountains!" explained Anchorin, peering into the distance.
Everyone also looked afar, to see the pale blue silhouettes on the horizon.
"Will the hoverbuggy go faster than this?" asked Sarah.
"Just a little bit more, but not advisable except for short bursts, as its hovering capacity soon loses power, and the buggy will just come to a halt and need to recharge itself for half an hour, at least," replied Anchorin.
"That's alright, I just wondered," said Sarah, "the countryside is so beautiful, and I'm not in a hurry!"
The others agreed, for they looked around constantly, viewing everything they passed. Kenny exclaimed as a Pegasus flew up into the sky over a wood on their right.
"That was the wood I visited with you Jadeir, and met your friends," he said, looking at Jadeir and then at the others.
"There's an arching light over that wood," said Karin, pointing, "what is it, Anchorin?"
"That is the energy coming from a little temple that some of the priests from both the main temple in Chalidocea, and our mountain temple set up together. They do good work in helping to distribute good energy, both via the ley lines and individual places," replied Anchorin.
"Are there other temples like this all over the land?" asked Alyssia.
"Yes indeed, there are many," responded Anchorin, "and all doing that energetic work. Even in a Golden Age work needs to be done!"
"Like gathering resources for times ahead, as well as enhancing the present Age to the best possible ability?" queried Sarah.
"Absolutely!" replied Anchorin, "you didn't need to ask!"
They continued onwards. The group periodically admired some beautiful trees or lake. The mountains were now very clear, and

lay only about twenty miles or so distant. The land became a little more alpine as they approached the mountains. There were lots of small tarns surrounded by low growing shrubs, and small, brightly coloured birds called to one another in the foliage.
"They are called Goura birds!" exclaimed Anchorin, "because their call sounds like that!"
"Oh yes! So it does!" responded Kenny.

Soon, they were skirting around the environs of the mountains, and came to a gushing spring.
"Ha! We'll stop here for something to eat, my friends!" announced Anchorin.
The others looked mildly puzzled, for there didn't appear to be any food. Anchorin smiled at their expressions.
"Well, here's the drink!" cried Anchorin, and then he looked at Jadeir meaningfully.
Jadeir dutifully jumped out of the buggy and gave a penetrating but melodious call that echoed around the area, like the continuous cry of a moorland bird's song. Within seconds, a group of elves, fairies and gnomes had gathered around, holding various bundles, tied up with leaves. They placed them down upon a rug that Anchorin had laid on the ground. The elementals all bowed and curtsied graciously.
"Your food awaits!" announced Jadeir.
The Oswestry group looked amazed, and thanked the elementals happily.
"You must have had this all arranged well in advance!" declared Kenny.
"We did indeed!" laughed Jadeir.
They all sat down to eat the provisions.

It was late evening in Atlantean time when they all arrived at the carved oak doors into the Garden of Eden. They were beautifully carved structures, with intertwining vines and other plants, which came alive when they were about to be opened. As Anchorin asked for the doors to open, the tall figure of Arwena appeared, who was the guardian there.
"Enter, my friends!" she uttered, her eyes glowing with an animated light. There was that pearly glow around her.
The doors came to life, and then unfurled their tendrils, so that the doors unlocked themselves, while the Oswestry group exclaimed in wonder. They all entered, and walked gently over the rich green grass, which never aged, nor needed cutting. Everyone was looking at the magnificent flora, iridescent sheens

shimmered over so many surfaces, and the fragrance of many of the flowers was essentially strong. They all realised that they were all glowing in pearly light too. A group of beings became apparent to them.
"Greetings, old friends!" they chorused, for they spoke as one being.
"Good day to you!" responded Anchorin, and he turned to the others, "this is the Sentinel."
The group smiled to them.
"Blessings be with you," replied Sarah, on behalf of their group.

After walking along peacefully through the length of the Garden, for the Oswestry group were so enamoured by the richness of it all, their eyes were absorbed in all they encountered.
"As you may recall, the Garden is so rich, since there is no winter here," reminded Anchorin.
"Oh yes, of course!" replied Alyssia and the others.
"Ah! The unicorns!" exclaimed Anchorin, and everyone turned their heads to see seven glowing horns appearing through the gentle mist that borders the Garden.
"Now we must fly over those large bushes to reach the centre," explained Anchorin, "and once over, we will see the temple on an island in the centre of the lake."

They all found themselves flying over the foliage that was by the temple and its surrounding lake, and they were accompanied by the Sentinel, but only to the water's edge.
"We must leave you now, for you are about to meet the three guardians of the alabaster jar," they said, "and the unicorns drew closer to Anchorin and the group, and there was an increase in energy and light, and they all rose up and gently glided over the water, over the grass of the temple grounds. The air was pure, and made everyone feel more alert and alive. They rose into the air and were across the water in a split second, it seemed, for time seemed to not exist there.
"Look! The colour of the water has changed!" exclaimed Alyssia.
They all turned to look.
"How incredible!" cried Sarah.
The water had turned a pale lilac, and an iridescent sheen was upon it, with golden flecks of light.
"It always does this when something important is about to happen," explained Anchorin, "and now the unicorns will accompany you to the temple, for I must leave you now."
Anchorin indicated for them to move in the direction of the temple, and enter the building. The group approached the

building gently, in silence, then turned to see Anchorin gliding over the water.

Chapter 6 – The Lore of the Legacy

They all entered the first vestibule of the glorious white temple, with its pink tinged base, and violet tinged dome, and whose marble-like stones held tiny pinpoints of sparkling golden light in them. It was like they were 'holding the sun', as the Oswestry group concluded afterwards. They also discovered that small pieces of gold and orichalcum had been inserted between the stones, so it wasn't just energy alone at work here.

Alyssia was positively radiant with the visual beauty everywhere, and had indicated for the others to look at the dome, for its surface was covered in a gold filigree tracery. Once inside, they felt the palpable calmness, and even the interior was intricately decorated.
"Perhaps we could make the shop interior up like this!" Kenny had commented afterwards.

They walked through gently; the light had a bluish tinge to it. Anchorin had told them to enter the next chamber after that. They all entered, and all heard a voice asking a question, simultaneously.
"Do you wish to help the earth for all time?"
The Oswestry group all affirmed that they did.
"Are your motives completely selfless? Came another voice.
They affirmed again.
"Are you strong enough?" came a third voice.
"We believe so," the group replied, "for we have served the high priests of Atlantis and the Council of Twelve."
"We see that you can be trusted," the voices said in unison, and a previously unseen door appeared.
"Please enter and proceed," and the group did.
They looked around at each other, and noticed that a projection of Anchorin was there, just watching. Kenny was glancing around, just in case Hudlath may have been projecting his image too, but there was only Anchorin, and then the image faded after a moment. The room they were in became dark and cool, and the group instinctively drew closer together. An image appeared on the wall in front of them. At first they couldn't make it out, for its imagery changed and transformed like a kaleidoscope. One moment it was like leafy patterns, and another was like many insects in formation, and there were endless other varieties. Then they all gradually noticed that the formations were so patterned that a face could be seen within them, irrespective of whichever pattern was now appearing.

Then the patterns faded, just leaving the impression of the face, in question.

"Greetings, my friends!" came a bright and joyful voice.

The group gave their greetings in return.

"I have a task for you all to achieve. Are you willing to try? If so, step forward now," said the voice.

The group all stepped forward, and the voice sounded very pleased.

"Please come," continued the voice, and an image of timeless beauty permeated the group. The darkness and cold vanished like shadows at dawn, and there, revealed, was a pearl coloured room, such as Anchorin had seen when he came for the casket, and the room was filled with gentle music. In the centre was the circular pedestal table, made of marble, and was four feet in diameter. A marble container stood upon it, with gold coloured edging.

"Please approach and lift the lid, one of you," continued the voice.

Alyssia was the one who lifted the lid, revealing the intense and powerful energy and light that emanated from it. Everyone closed their eyes, as it was so powerful, as Anchorin had done. After a few minutes, the group managed to open their eyes to a degree.

"Now, please lift out the inner casket that holds the essence," said the voice.

Karin came and lifted it out, holding it a moment, while the others gathered around.

"I wish to anoint you all, so please remain where you are," instructed the voice again.

The lid of the white casket holding the essence began to rise slowly, and a portion of the essence floated over to Karin's forehead, and she felt a finger rubbing it on. Then more of it went to Alyssia's forehead to rub it on, and then to Kenny and Sarah. They all began to see a mass of colour swirling around themselves, and then they could see the three guardians of the casket and temple.

Kenny looked puzzled, and thought 'where is Jadeir?' and then his expression became brighter, for he knew immediately that Jadeir had just disappeared and returned with Anchorin, and that they were both monitoring progress with the group, while back at the mountain temple.

Alyssia instantly knew that the three beings before them were closely linked with Gaia, as did Sarah. Karin knew they also linked with the sacred goddess energy.

"Greetings, I am Anui, who anointed you all," stated the first being.

"I am Deanu," said the second being.

"And I am Giana," said the third being.

The three beings drew up close, and looked at the Oswestry group.

"You do know us, indeed!" and their voices sounded like a chord. The group could see images of a mountainous land, waterfalls with oracular priests and priestesses around them, advising people. People only lived in small villages or caves, sharing their lives together in harmony, and didn't need to eat much. They could see the three beings there, singing in unison, and it was as if they had been singing throughout the Earth's time period and all of time.

"You know we link closely with Gaia, and two of you have met her, and yes, you know we are the fulcrum of the planet. You must take some sips of the essence now," said Anui.

The three goddess-like guardians had skin that was like sparkling pearly light, over alabaster, yet with a shining radiance that emanated from inside them. Their clothing was diaphanous, in shades of green-blues, with sparkling diamonds, emeralds and sapphires over gold and silver filigree embroidery. They had hair that was piled up on top of their heads, and cascaded down their necks too. There was music that emanated from them constantly.

Karin stepped forward to take the first sips. Her eyes went blurry momentarily, and then back into focus. She saw images of the old world of Lemuria, while the eyes were blurry, as well as older times of Atlantis. Also, how the people had been more ethereal at times, kind and gentle, and at others, weighed down by the successive Kali Ages, and had become confused, corrupted and soulless. She could see to the origins of man, his first steps onto Mother Earth as an ethereal being who was not incarnated into a physical world, and therefore, did not know Earthly cares, and who had no verbal language, and spent a lot of time just exploring their world, linking with other ethereal beings such as elementals, guides, and beings from other worlds who visited frequently.

"May the next person come forward," requested Anui.

Kenny indicated for Alyssia to be the next one, and she approached and took some sips of the essence. She found herself immediately in the presence of Gaia.
"Remember Alyssia, remember..." came the words.
Somehow, it moved her greatly, and as she came to and looked around at the others, her eyes were filled with tears.
"It was Gaia, asking me to remember something..." she explained, "I wish I could."
Anui, Deanu and Giana looked at her compassionately.
"You will recall, my friend," responded Deanu, "just know that memory will come."
"Now that you have drunk the essence," added Giana.
The three guardians looked around expectantly for the next person. Kenny graciously let Sarah go next. She took sips, and her face took on a deeply thoughtful expression, and her eyes became animated.
"I can see the origins of the love of wise men and women for living in caves as going back to before Lemuria, when people were more ethereal, and so they didn't feel the cold. You know, I can also see further back to a time when they were on other planets and living in this way."
"That is very true, Sarah," remarked Deanu, "there is so much learnt while living in such simple abodes."

Sarah moved away, allowing Kenny to come forward. He took the sips of essence, and saw many iridescent colours forming, and a piercing light began to appear, and he shielded his eyes, but couldn't do so effectively, because the light was from inside. A force of energy came upwards through him, and then he saw images of beings from far afield. He wondered where they were from, and then he knew, from many star systems and galaxies. There was so much energy that he thought he must be either airborne or burning a hole in the temple floor. Anui, Deanu and Giana smiled at his thoughts, and then the light became gentler, and he began to move slowly.
"Wow! That was really powerful!" uttered Kenny.
"We could all see the bright energy around you, Kenny," said the others in the Oswestry group.
"That must have been the kundalini, why didn't any of you have that?" he asked, curiously.
"Don't be so sure you are the odd one out," advised Anui, "sometimes it is imperceptible, and sometimes it comes in a huge powerful rush!"
"What must we do now?" asked Sarah.

Anui and Deanu looked thoughtful, while Giana was conducting a small ceremony at the far side of the temple. A slow, gentle smile spread over their faces, with a suggestion to wait and see. The group stood and watched Giana at work. She had her back to everyone, and was softly chanting, while putting sacred herbs to the goddess of the temple in a chalice-shaped burner. As the group watched, each one felt a depth of purpose, why they had been drawn to come, why their lives had brought them to this point, and there was a growing sense of being included into the depths of what the goddess wished them to know, and also to be.

The whole of the temple space became filled with a shimmering light, like the light that emanates from candles, but also when reflecting on the surface of water. The group felt drawn to move into the centre of the temple area. Anui and Deanu each moved over to where Giana was at work, but they positioned themselves either side, and with a few feet apart from each other. Then the Oswestry group were aware that all three of the guardians had lit small fires and incenses, and the temple was becoming filled with the heady aromas.

The guardians began to move around within a circle, and indicated for the group to follow them. Then, after a few times around the circle, the group were invited to pause at each of the altar fires, inhale the heady scent, and then slowly walk around the circle again.

After some moments of feeling disorientated, they became aware of a glowing presence in the centre of the circle, and a figure was forming in front of them all. The figure was female and she was smiling. Everyone in the Oswestry group smiled in return once they realised who it was.
"Mother Gaia!" exclaimed Alyssia and Sarah in an excited whisper.
"Yes, I am Gaia, my friends. I know you have anticipated my visit for a while. I am going to give you a task to do that will help our planet."
Gaia paused in her speech a moment, looking around at them all, as if to draw out their thoughts somewhat. Her pale blond hair and white clothing took on a green-blue tinge, reflecting the Earth's seas, and the group's reflection later, were convinced they could see the movement of waves within it.
"How can we help you and our planet, Gaia?" asked Alyssia.
"What gifts do you all possess?" she responded.

With those words uttered, everyone began to find themselves in a meditative state, seeing symbols, visions, and listening to inner wisdom. Finally, everything was concluded, and the light around the temple area that had been shimmering during the whole ceremony, quietened down. Anui, Deanu and Giana invited the group to sit on a seated area to the far side of the temple, opposite the altars. Gaia also came over to join them.

"I feel I must use my healing skills more fully," stated Sarah, and her face brightened, "I know how to use the old Atlantean herbs. Are there other seeds I can take back with us to grow?"

"Indeed there are! Go and visit the temple gardens in Chalidocea if you wish. However, we have a good selection here at this temple," responded Deanu, "we will show you!"

Gaia nodded approvingly.

"I have been writing the Atlantean story, and of course I paint as well," began Alyssia, "perhaps I can contribute to whatever the others are doing to form something together. Though I don't know what that will be yet."

"My friend, think of what healing art, writing and spirituality could do to enhance your skills. Writing the Atlantean story will help further your gifts," responded Gaia.

Karin glanced thoughtfully over to the altar, and then looked at the group.

"I'm not entirely sure what I can contribute as yet, because Kenny and I just run the shop, and there's not a lot of extra time left. Though I used to make pots when Alyssia and I were both living in Cumbria."

"No, it won't be making pottery," said Gaia, "did you see anything in your meditation at all?"

"Well, I saw a star, and a being came into vision, and then faded away," replied Karin, "I wonder who it was."

She paused a moment, and then her face became animated.

"You know! I think it was indicating channelling!"

"You are right! It was a gift you used in Atlantis, my friend, soon to be regenerated!"

Karin laughed with delight, "how wonderful!"

Everyone smiled at Karin's response, and then turned to look at Kenny, and he gave his usual comical stare and shrugged.

"Hey! Well, I did see something in my meditation, and saw myself talking with people, but I do that quite a bit anyway in the shop," replied Kenny.

"Yes, that is so my friend," said Gaia, "but you can do more than just have chats to people, you know it inside."

Kenny pondered a moment, and thought over his meditation again. "Oh yes, there was a split second appearance of me

standing in front of an audience in a lecture room, I'd quite forgotten! How could I have forgotten that?"
"There you have it!" cried Gaia, "a good team in the making I see before me!" and she smiled jovially.

"Well, I'd love to see that herb garden, can I now?" asked Sarah.
"How can I get going with the channelling?" asked Karin.
"Alright!" laughed Anui, Deanu and Giana, and they ushered everyone through to behind the temple.
Gaia was still with them, her white robes glowing brightly. Once outside, her face that had been quite mature, was now revealed as youthful, with her long fair hair now gathered upon her head, and ringlets cascading down at the back, and across her right cheek, her eyes were glowing animatedly.

"Come and see these herbs!" cried Anui, "the one here with star-shaped leaves is called Venus Starflower because it holds the energy of all the elements. We will explain! It was the most sacred of herbs and only found on Atlantis, unfortunately, though it was once shared with the rest of the world," explained Anui.
"Were there not priests in other parts of the world to ensure worldwide supplies?" asked Alyssia.
"There were; it is a long story, as most are!" commented Deanu, "when all was harmonious all over the world; the sacred herbs were found worldwide, having been shared and held in the temples and gardens, as very sacred, and treated with great care. The plants were also shared with many groups of good intent, and all was well. When the Golden Age languished, so did the habits of the human population, as expected, and soon enough the sacred herbs were being used for other purposes, though in many places they went neglected. Many plants died out altogether, and we know from an ancient record that certain priests of good intent travelled around to find any remaining sacred herbs to take any seeds, and if possible, uproot the plants and take them away. It seems they were very successful despite the huge task, for they had the many nature spirits to inform them of the plants whereabouts."
Anui handled an adjacent plant, and gestured for the Oswestry group to look at it.
"This one is different indeed, for the starflower helps a priest's clairsentient abilities through balance and harmony, while this plant did what?"
Anui stopped speaking abruptly and looked at Sarah.

Sarah's expression immediately became thoughtful, with a penetrating depth to it, and then a look of comprehension passed over her face.

"The galaxy plant!" cried Sarah, "because it helps a person travel to other planets to gain knowledge, which can be given to Earth."

"That was information well received!" replied Anui, "yes, it could bring a universal frequency to an individual."

"What became of all those herbs?" asked Sarah, "despite the priesthood managing to save the herb seed at certain times?"

"Eventually the herbs died out on this planet," said Giana, with a faraway, pensive look, "the plants were thought to have no further use with the majority of people here, even many priests and priestesses intuited that it would be safer for the plants to return to their true homes, and perhaps return to Earth when times become harmonious once more, possibly."

"However, you can gain from seeing the plants here, and know that the wisdom gained can never be lost from you," explained Anui, and she smiled with a sparkle in her eyes, "you know, in due course, plants will be discovered in certain places with these qualities, just wait and see!"

"That sounds lovely!" responded Sarah emphatically, "whereabouts? Do you know?"

Giana smiled again, "I'm sorry, but I have to keep that information just to ourselves."

"Oh, I understand," responded Sarah, "are there any more plants to see?"

"I should have known you would ask!" laughed Giana, and she turned to look at Anui and Deanu; they began to laugh too. "Come on everyone! You'll find out what the joke is soon enough."

They all walked away from the medicine plant area, down a leafy path, and into a thick, forested area. The Oswestry group looked around themselves with slightly concerned expressions.

"Don't worry, this forest is very peaceful and quiet," responded Anui, "except for beautiful birdsong."

Within a short time they were going uphill, the forest becoming rapidly less dense. Suddenly they were in the open air, with a view stretching for miles over the viridian canopy, with mountain peaks visible through the greenery at intervals, which echoed the periodic melodious sounds of the Goura birds, as well as some other curious sounding birds. Kenny and Karin had asked Anui what the elusive, lovely and delicate, almost whispering song was coming from, and sounded like someone speaking very rapidly in a half melodic manner. They were the Gossamer Speech birds and only to be found in this forest.

The group continued up along the mountainous forest path a little while longer to another promontory, which overlooked a cascading waterfall. The sound of the water was so loud, everyone had to use other means to communicate with each other.

Anui and Deanu pointed over to an aperture beside the waterfall, and they all clambered over to it. The group realised as they approached, that the aperture was a cave, and the path came to an end about five feet short of the cave entrance. The group definitely looked apprehensive now.

"Remember you can hover!" reminded Deanu, "we've seen you do it! Just because there's a huge drop here makes no difference really, you know!"

"Yes, we know in theory," replied Sarah, "It's just that we haven't had as much practice as birds!"

"Now's your chance! Go on! It's truly safe!" cried Anui, "watch me!"

Anui floated across effortlessly, and then flew back to the group.

"Come on Sarah, remember that plant you wished to see," cried Deanu, taking Sarah's arm, and she began to rise a couple of inches. Sarah grasped her crystal and focused, and then she began to rise as well, and they were soon across the chasm of white foaming water.

Kenny took Karin's arm, they took hold of their wands, and then they both floated across. Kenny turned and yelled to the remaining Alyssia and Giana, "come on over, the water's lovely!"

Alyssia smiled and grasped her crystal wand too, looked at Giana and began to rise upwards, and Giana did the same, and then in synchronised movement, they both moved gracefully over the water and landed gently beside the others.

"Well done everyone!" said Anui, "now, let's move along this passageway a little, to a point when I shall stop, then we will go up some steps."

Sarah and Alyssia found themselves walking together. They looked at each other in a meaningful way, and both knew each of them was thinking of their experiences on Lemuria, inside the obsidian caves.

Where they stopped was at a quiet and roomy area of the cave, and then each of them knew that the steps were close by. The steps they took lead them up in a slow spiral. As they climbed, the light became less dim again, as they rose to another roomy area, and then Deanu indicated another cave route.

"I hope this plant is worth seeing!" commented Kenny, and Karin gave him a slightly scolding look, and he responded with an innocent glance.

Inside the entrance to the cave they all paused for a moment. Kenny nudged Karin, as he could feel something brushing his face and neck. Karin reached to grasp whatever it was, and found it was only a frond hanging from the side of the cave.

Anui and Deanu put their fingers over their mouths as they looked at the group, and then beckoned for them to follow. They promptly turned a corner and disappeared. The group looked at each other, perplexed.

"It's a dead end, what's going on!" cried Kenny.

"Giana's gone too!" cried Alyssia.

"How could they leave us here?" said Sarah.

"Look everyone, what's this here?" commented Karin, and she went over to look.

A luminescent glow was beginning to appear on one of the walls. The group all went to watch it. A high-pitched sound like a chant came into everyone's minds, but somehow sung by non-human voices. It was difficult for the group to describe that sound, but it was moving and inspiring, and lifted them away from any former distress.

The glow increased and sparkled brightly, and could be seen around the edges of leaves and flowers of a plant growing on the cave's walls. Sarah and Alyssia went to touch the leaves, and it was as if they became linked to the plant, also becoming iridescent and sparkling as well.

Alyssia saw herself rushing at very high speeds through space, and there, a planet covered in iridescent plants and trees, with people that sparkled with a light of their own, as well as their clothes. All was very peaceful. Suddenly a face came close to Alyssia's.

"Valana, awaken my friend!" Then the image faded away. Alyssia turned to Sarah, "I saw the same as you, Alyssia, but the person called me Salana!"

"It was Astragandara, Sarah, I know it!"

Tears were trickling down Alyssia's face, and now Sarah's.

Kenny came over and gave Sarah and Alyssia a big hug, with an arm around each of them, and then Karin joined in.

"You're great friends, even if you didn't come from Astragandara!" said Sarah, and Alyssia agreed.

"Perhaps we came from one nearby!" suggested Karin, jovially.

"Yeah, the one with Tesco's on it!" quipped Kenny, and they all laughed, "by the way, is it alright to ask what you two saw?"
Alyssia and Sarah related their visions.
"We wish we could see what needs awakening, and how to do it, and thought what we did with Gaia was what we needed to do," commented Alyssia.
"Awaken Valana and Salana," cried Kenny.
A strange echoing began within the short tunnel area, the names echoed and re-echoed. Kenny gave an astonished look, indicative of not having wished to start anything so dramatic. Alyssia and Sarah had to sit down, their hands to their heads, and they crouched down with their eyes shut, and leant their heads against the cave wall. Karin and Kenny stood nearby, unable to hear the sounds any more, as they had just faded away. Kenny gave Karin a concerned look.
"What can we do? What's going on?" he uttered.
"All we can do is stand by and wait," replied Karin.

A green figure appeared in the cave entrance and touched Karin and Kenny on their arms, and looked into their eyes. They both felt strange, and their vision became blurred, and they had to sit down as well. The figure exuded gentle love and peace, but they couldn't move, and it was as if all the energy of nature came inside them, filling their consciousness with that of the whole planet. Suddenly there was a vast green pathway leading off the planet to a very verdant planet, covered in sparkling sea-green crystals, with green people wandering around. A strong energy permeated Karin and Kenny.

The group all came to at the same time; looked at each other and smiled.
"Yes, we have remembered, Kenny, Karin!" responded Alyssia excitedly, and she looked at Sarah too, who was smiling happily.
"I think I know where we've come from too," replied Karin.
"Indeed! It's Verdamara of course!" cried Kenny.
"What about that luminous plant, I wonder what it's called?" pondered Alyssia.
"The Hall of Memories plant, of course!" replied Sarah, her face holding a hint of humour, as well as bright inspiration.

Chapter 7 – Embarkation to Verdamara

The Oswestry group along with Anui, Deanu and Giana had returned to the timeless looking log cabin that the priestesses of the Garden of Eden lived in. The outside of the dwelling was covered in bright green mosses, and feeding trays for the Goura birds outside the windows, mainly reachable from the living room, and the kitchen area.

Looking out to the starry, clear and open skies of Atlantis in the Golden Age, they were all silent for a while; having watched the sunset's final glow on the far horizon, over the lilac shaded mountainous silhouettes.
"Which mountains are those on the horizon, Anui?" asked Sarah, softly, not wishing to break the silent reverie they were participating in too much.
Anui's eyes reflected the starlight, for the stars were much brighter in those times, for the Earth herself was closer to the centre of the universe, away from the influences from less advanced planets and constellations, which she had to reacquaint herself to periodically, however.
"They are the Diorama Peaks, my friend, filled with precious gems," answered Anui.
"Has anyone utilised any of those gems from there, or anywhere else?" asked Alyssia, "I know you have your healing crystals of course, but they could have been handed down over centuries, perhaps?"
"Yes, the principle on Atlantis at present, is that we know we can use a certain amount of gems and minerals, and the rest is allowed to remain the property of the planet," explained Anui; "we are guided by Gaia on this matter."
"The reason why, is that the soil is enriched by the presence of these gems and minerals," commented Giana.
"That sound most sensible and right," concurred Alyssia, and she looked out at the distant peaks, and she was aware of seeing some of those peaks as if magnified, and could see giant crystals several yards in diameter, shining out of the sides of those peaks, with an inner light.

Later, Alyssia slipped into a starlit dream of reaching towards richly sparkling emerald-hued crystals, and finding herself in a chamber held within the mountain, where people were sat in a circular formation in high-backed seats. They were deep in discussion. In a vacant place, Alyssia was invited to sit, and she immediately understood that they were in the next dimension and oversaw the Atlantean culture, monitoring its progress and needs.

"We have held council for millennia, although different people take over these positions at various times, in the way people do on Earth in the physical world," said a friendly, bearded man to Alyssia's right, "my name is Arlando."

"Have you lived on Earth during that Atlantean time period before taking this position, Arlando?" asked Alyssia.

"I have lived in the early era of Atlantis, and others here have lived in Lemuria," here he paused with an emphatic look, "and even earlier than that! We would advise the general populace, and do what we could to ensure that the race was guided thoroughly, because their minds were not developed before the Lemurian race, and needed a lot of guidance in many ways. Even in the Lemurian period, help was needed, though there was an increase of proportion towards more intellectual people, even though they wouldn't be thought of as exceptional in your time," and his eyes twinkled merrily.

"That's why there are less elders apparent now?" asked Alyssia, "of course there are some sages and avatars in India and elsewhere, but perhaps not as prevalent as then, is that so?"

"Yes indeed, the elders and mentors were apparent all over the world at one time, until the Atlantean culture began, and then there was a gradual retreat, because the elders knew man had to now fulfil his own destiny in his own way, independently to a greater degree," explained Arlando.

"Will they become more prevalent again?" asked Alyssia.

Arlando smiled knowingly, "it is the intention that man takes the steps in order to become self-reliant, and a true guardian of the planet. The way all other three dimensional planets have had to evolve, by being guided for a while, and then left more increasingly to their own devices. A bit like raising children, though I don't want to sound condescending, because it is an arduous journey, and us elders are not too far away really, and watch from afar frequently. In fact, to be honest, we did prefer it when we were with you all constantly, like many parents; it is an anxious time leaving children to take those steps out in the world, and many is the time when we have wanted to go and help, but we have given our word to the law that we have to follow certain procedures.

"What about people who receive channelled information? That is offering help, is it not?" asked Alyssia.

"Yes indeed! We are allowed to give a little help now and again! It depends on the individual, and not all channelling comes directly from a Master, for it may be from a disciple or follower

working for a Master or Elder, who is in fact allowed to pass messages through a back door route. A bit of an unwritten rule or clause!" explained Arlando, and he chuckled jovially.
"I think I've spoken enough, my friend. We have business to attend to now!" said Arlando, smiling broadly.
"Yes, I think it is time for me to awake. Thank you very much, I've enjoyed coming to the Diorama Peaks," responded Alyssia.

They waved to each other, and elders in the other seats smiled kindly, and then Alyssia rose upwards and out of the mountain. She saw the sparkling emerald crystals again on the mountain's surface, and she could see some of those crystals inside the mountain too, emanating energies very strongly, and radiating it all around the countryside, and within the Earth's structure.
'A mountain could be considered to be part of a chakra system, as a point for generating energy to a greater degree, and as a nadi if to a lesser degree,' thought Alyssia.
'Quite right too!' came that thought to Alyssia, accompanied by the image of Arlando's face. Alyssia smiled in response.

The morning light was very bright, and a myriad of Goura birds, it seemed to Alyssia, were calling out at the windows of the cabin, their bright plumage with a glossy sheen reflecting the sunlight in tiny sparkles. Alyssia saw some figures at the window, and she turned to look at Sarah, for Karin and Kenny were in the next room and the figures called to them.
"Greetings and welcome to the new day, in the land of Eden!" sang the three figures dressed in shimmering light clothing. Their appearance was entirely a spring green colour, reflected a green light, and were fairy-like in appearance.
"Hello!" responded Alyssia and Sarah.
"We know your group are here for a purpose!" they said.
"What do you perceive that we are to do?" asked Sarah.
"Do you understand what you will do with your gifts you possess?" asked one of the figures.
"Excuse me!" said another of the beings, "we have not been introduced to each other yet, it isn't correct to talk at length, when these people do not know whom we are!"
The other two beings agreed.
"Our names are Leandra, Elandera and Salandra, and we have lived here at the Garden of Eden for many centuries. We like to help and advise those who visit!" said Elandera, and she indicated who each of them were.
"We are glad to meet you!" cried Salandra.

"We know what you are going to do next!" stated Leandra, with a slight smile.

"What are we going to do?" asked Alyssia.

A shimmering green light with golden sparkles and striations running through it appeared around them all.

Sarah and Alyssia looked at each other.

"You know! I think we are meant to visit Verdamara," said Sarah.

"I think so too. Let's ask the others!" agreed Alyssia, "though I think they already know!"

"They certainly do, as we have just visited Karin and Kenny a few moments ago!" cried Leandra.

With that, the three nature spirits laughed cheerfully, and Alyssia and Sarah responded as well.

"What is it that we are to do on Verdamara?" asked Karin, looking at the others in the group, later on that morning.

"I think we have something to do that involves drawing information to bring back to Earth, and share something with those on Verdamara in return," mused Kenny.

"Yes, that sounds right, though I'm not sure what we can share at present," responded Sarah.

"Why not meditate on it!" suggested Alyssia.

"Ok!" responded Sarah, giving Alyssia a penetrating look, but shouldn't we visit Astragandara also?"

"We can visit them both, why not!" said Kenny, "as we need to know everything we can."

Giana knocked on the door to Kenny and Karin's room where they were all talking.

"Hello, come and join us a moment!" she called.

Everyone came out to see what was happening. Deanu smilingly presented them with a delicious looking fruit cocktail repast, freshly picked from their garden, and accompanied by an effervescent drink, which had an aroma of exotic fruit as well.

"This will energise you for your journeys!" exclaimed Deanu.

"We know you are going to visit your two native planets of origin, therefore this will sustain you, and your transport will be arriving fairly soon!" said Anui.

"My! You are organised!" responded Sarah.

There were sounds of light-hearted chuckles all round as the Oswestry group sat to their small meal, while the three guardian sisters watched on.

"I didn't expect this fruit would give much energy, it certainly doesn't back home. You can really feel the energy surging through!" exclaimed Kenny brightly, having finished his portion.

"You're so right!" agreed Karin, and the other two echoed her comments.

They all ventured to try the drink.

"Powerful!" cried Kenny, with an incredulous look.

"I can see the energies of the different plants that have gone into it, all the sacred ones we have seen in the garden, including the Venus Starflower and the Galaxy Plant," said Sarah, thoughtfully, "and I think the seeds have been used in it, along with Eden spring waters."

"Well spotted my friend!" responded Deanu.

The image of the caskets' disks flashed across Alyssia's mind's eye.

"I've just seen an image of the caskets' disks, I wonder if they link in here," explained Alyssia, "after all, we never got to seeing what was on them."

"That's true," responded Sarah, "I wonder if they need to be viewed by us now."

"Either before or after our journeys," added Karin.

There was the familiar sound of a spaceship alighting nearby.

"Come on! Let's get ready!" cried Kenny, "no more speculation required for now!" and they went off to gather their belongings.

The craft took off with the Oswestry group aboard, alongside the spaceship occupants of Zanadar, Aurion and Salaron, from Cassiopeia, Sirius and the Pleiades respectively. Siral, Golan and Maeron were also aboard, from Andromeda, Arcturus and the Hyades, in turn, and they were working in other parts of the craft. The Oswestry group had telepathic contact with the three sisters in Eden for a while, and talked with them via the screen in the general control room, where everyone sat if they wished or needed to, and there was the large window screen to view the journey route.

"Astragandara and Verdamara are both near the centre of our universe, so they are relatively close together," explained Zanadar, speaking a little louder than usual, to catch the attention of those in the Oswestry group who were talking to the three sisters. His orange-pink face had a cheerful expression, as usual.

"Is it true that the spaceship speeds up naturally, the nearer to the centre of the universe we go?" asked Kenny.

"Yes, it is true, because the pull of the lower planes, i.e. the third and fourth dimensions begin to lose their grip, and so..." at this Zanadar gave a quizzical look and paused.

The rest of the Oswestry group, who were just concluding their talks with the three sisters in Eden, turned their heads attentively to consider the reason for the pause.

"Does that mean," began Sarah, "that we lose our connection with the lower dimensions too?"

"Correct, you will be lifted up as a matter of course," replied Zanadar.

"Will we go right to the centre or nearby?" asked Kenny, "because are we able to encounter the sixth and seventh dimensions that lie closer to the centre, or will we presumably remain in the fifth dimension where we're going to?"

"Good question!" responded Zanadar, "we shall approach the outer ring, but it is considered as part of the centre. So we will only encounter the fifth dimension, the other two are not for you all, yet!"

"I suppose Earth in our time will continue in our wake, as she is on her return journey towards the centre of the universe, slowly," commented Alyssia.

"She certainly is, although if you could see how fast she is travelling, you would not say slow! Though the material universe is quite vast," said Zanadar.

"Could you compare the universe to a cellular body, in that you have the exterior wall representing the physical level, various electrons etc representing the fourth dimension, and the spaces between as the higher levels," explained Karin.

"Perhaps," responded Zanadar, "or even the Bhuta kasha, Chitta kasha and Chida kasha levels, as they say in India, being the physical level, emotional and mental level, and the higher mental and Buddhic level in turn, which actually correspond to the third, fourth and fifth onwards, dimensions."

He then accelerated the craft by pushing a lever forwards. The group could see masses of pinpoints of light ahead of them.

"You'd better get prepared, my friends," explained Aurion, "because the next half an hour in your time will be gone soon, and we shall be entering a zone that holds fourth dimensional energy, and your bodies will have to cope."

"If you would like to follow me," announced Salaron, "I shall take you to the healing rooms, where Siral and Maeron await, and this will help you."

Down the corridor they all went, and were treated to the view of a splendid healing room.

"I've never seen such a place! It looks even more impressive than the one in the temple at Chalidocea!" exclaimed Sarah.

"Yes, these crystal beds are geared up to higher frequencies than on Earth, that is why," explained Siral, "and even we need treatment periodically, since we often travel between one universe in the Kali Age, to another in another Age, and so on. Of course, reaching to the sixth dimension, and then going off to a third or fourth dimensional plane and back again can be most tiring for the constitution."

Maeron approached Karin and Kenny, and indicated for them to go through to another room that was just the same.

"There is only room for two in each healing room, so let's go!" said Maeron.

Alyssia and Sarah, meanwhile, were invited to lie down on a crystal bed each. Sarah began to smile and whispered to Alyssia.

"I can't help thinking of the bed that Hudlath accidentally pressed the wrong button on, and nearly folded up inside it!"

"Oh yes, that was hilarious," laughed Alyssia, with her hand over her mouth.

Siral overheard and smiled, "I heard about that!"

The light became muted and the crystals began to glow brightly, and everyone in the Oswestry group could feel the energy working through them strongly. Siral was working on Sarah at that moment, and Alyssia could see them glowing, and could see herself glowing also. Siral knew that Maeron was doing the same as he was with Karin and Kenny. They both waited for a specific increase in energy levels before going on to the next stage. Taking some laser crystals, he made symbolic insignia in the air about Sarah and Alyssia, and talking quietly to the crystal in a timeless language, dating back to ancient times when priesthoods first began to work with crystals, and were handed the meanings of much from visitors from other star systems. As a result of his incantation, the laser crystal arced bright lights of opalescent hues and sparkling diamond-like brilliance, and this energy wrapped itself around them like a cocoon. Siral knew it would send them into what seemed like a deep sleep, but in fact it would be an energy reconstitution, taking them to the correct frequency to meet this part of their universe they were about to enter. He focussed his mind on Zanadar, as to how long it would be before the pale green light in the realms of space would begin to dawn, and then the two groups of planets would be discernable, one of which held the destination of Verdamara.

Sarah and Alyssia began stirring, and Siral indicated a rejuvenating drink for them, once they got up. It stood on a nearby table, which lay between their two crystal beds.

"That was so relaxing!" said Sarah.

"Yes it certainly was, although I found that I was able to see what was going on in the ship, even though we were both either asleep or unconscious. You know, I saw other beings on board, all kinds, as if they were coming from different parts of the universe for certain reasons, and we aren't normally aware of the fact it may happen all the time. Is that so?" remarked Alyssia.

"Indeed you have perceived well, my friend," responded Siral, giving a warm smile, "there are many other beings from the higher dimensions travelling with us, and especially so now we are reaching the higher frequency levels in this universe, and it won't be long now!"

Sarah and Alyssia began sipping the proffered drinks, and Siral wrapped up the crystals, and also tidied up the room.

"I can feel a strong glow going through the whole of me," exclaimed Sarah, "I think it's increasing in strength!"

"I can feel it too!" cried Alyssia, "it's definitely like a burst of kundalini. Gosh!"

Siral looked attentive and came to their sides.

"I think you two should lie down again for a short while, until this surge of energy has passed by. It should only take a few minutes," he explained.

In the main deck's steering area of the control room, Zanadar looked out at the screen, searching for the signs of an approaching 'dawn' of green light. As he peered, a tiny area of pale green appeared in the centre, growing gradually bigger as they progressed. He concentrated to send the message to Siral and Maeron that the fifth dimension was quite close.

After fifteen minutes has passed, the Oswestry group came through into the control room, and Zanadar ushered them to the seating area.

"There are hot drinks available for you, here!" announced Zanadar. He indicated to the other side of the room, and then focused on the drinks machine, and it poured out four drinks into cups that moved under the spout on a little conveyer belt. Alyssia went to fetch them, for the cups were now on a small tray.

Although the temperature on the ship was comfortably warm, the hot drinks were welcomed by the group, due to their energy change. They all began to focus on the approaching patch of pale green light, as they sipped their hot drinks.

"Take especial notice of what happens next!" announced Zanadar.

Just then, Siral and Maeron entered.

"We just love to come and watch, you'll see!" exclaimed Siral.

They came to sit by the Oswestry group.

Sure enough, the increasing light began to spangle, and streams of glittering sparkles radiated outwards, all around. Also, a myriad of rainbow streaks and prismatic shapes danced everywhere. There was a humming sound at a fairly low pitch, which increased in volume as well as pitch. This had a dramatic effect on the rainbow streaks and glittering sparkles, and made them all merge into a huge mass of shimmering golden and opalescent light, that framed the area of pale green light.

"That's so beautiful!" cried Alyssia, "I'll paint that!"

"Oh yes, how splendid!" responded Karin. The other two, Sarah and Kenny looked appreciative and smiled in agreement.

"It hasn't finished yet!" remarked Siral.

As the green light with golden and opalescent surroundings came even closer, so that the ship was about to pass through this formation, the whole ship became immersed in that golden and opalescent light, so that everything shimmered around them.

"We are all shimmering too!" Alyssia softly whispered.

All of them then felt unable to speak, due to this high frequency running through them, bringing a sense of brilliance into their mien, shedding any lack of energy or insight, characterised by having been in the third and fourth dimensional parts of the universe.

The Oswestry group looked over to Zanadar, and exclaimed in surprise, as a dozen beings had appeared beside him.

Siral smiled, "there! Your dream has become true, Alyssia!"

"Yes!" she replied, "where are they from, Siral?"

Siral waited until all of the Oswestry group were listening.

"From Verdamara and surrounding planets," the group looked delighted, "you'll meet them in a moment."

The group studied the figures closely, intrigued by the translucent and pearly skin they had; some were flesh coloured with that effect, and others were pale spring green. The ones with flesh coloured skin had clothes that were pale pink and the green skinned ones wore spring green, with a golden and silver sheen to them. They approached the Oswestry group, having finished their discussion with Zanadar. Some of the green skinned ones were walking over to them initially, in a graceful manner; they had very expressive faces that were refined, with eyes that radiated light.

"Hello friends, we are from Verdamara and welcome you all. We shall be landing soon!" said one.

"Our names are Ramusa, Larana and Salusa, and I am Ramusa!" said another.

They all laughed because they knew that as they looked so similar, like all on Verdamara, the Oswestry group would have endless trouble wondering who was who. The group intuited why they were laughing and began to join in!

Then some of the beings dressed in pink came over next, and also looked similar to each other and in mien.

"We are from Reluisia, the adjacent planet to Verdamara, and we both share our resources, of a planetary nature, as well as knowledge and wisdom," she explained, "my name is Leana, and the other three are Galaya, Enalda and Siraldah."

The Oswestry group exclaimed at the last name.

"Yes, there is a link to Siral, as you know he is from Andromeda, and at one time, some Andromedans came to share knowledge, as many of us exchange understanding, and they decided to stay with us. Our peoples are born by a kind of thought process by thinking and visualising hard, and the energy forms in our midst, and another being enters that thought form into the fifth dimension. Siral came to us that way, but he felt drawn to return to Andromeda," explained Leana.

"I am happy to visit you all again!" responded Siral.

By this time, a very bright green planet was becoming visibly larger, held in the vast sky of pale, bright green light.

The remaining beings who hadn't been introduced, smiled over to the Oswestry group, and then vanished.

"They've gone back to their planets to inform the others of our arrival," explained Siral, "we may see some of them later, let's prepare to disembark!"

The group, accompanied by Zanadar, Maeron and Siral, found Aurion and Salaron in the ante-chamber to the disembarking platform.

"Golan will be operating the platform's descent," explained Zanadar, "unfortunately you didn't see him this time, as he had a lot of maintenance to do."

"Was he doing it all himself?" asked Alyssia.

"No! We went to help while you all were receiving healing," responded Aurion, and he gestured to include Salaron.

"Send him our most cosmic love!" said Kenny.

"We will indeed!" chuckled Siral and the others.

With that, the antechamber door opened, and they all walked onto the platform that had a rail around it, which gently lowered them to the ground below. Zanadar opened the railing gate and invited everyone to step onto the planet. Needless to say that the Oswestry group were looking around themselves in amazement at the endless shades of green that was all around them.

"Look at those translucent and spangly leaves, Alyssia!" cried Karin.

"Yes, and look at these leaves here, they've all got patterns on in five shades of green, wow!" cried Alyssia.

Zanadar and the other space beings looked at each other with jovial smiles, seeing the group getting so excited about the greenery.

"Karin!" came the call from a clearing in the greenery.

Karin pricked up her ears and looked over alertly.

"The person in my vision!" and she hurried over to see the green female figure, dressed in the bright green long clothing that was customary to Verdamara. Kenny swiftly followed her.

"My name is Viridiana, do you remember me, both of you?"

"Yes I do," replied Karin, and she looked at Kenny.

"Yes," replied Kenny, and he gazed thoughtfully at Viridiana, as if he was trying to remember something.

"Why were we born on Earth instead of remaining here?" he asked.

"Because you decided to interlink our two cultures together, and by remembering us, you could then begin to do so, and bring in good things that would help Earth," explained Viridiana.

"Have you brought a notebook, Karin?" asked Kenny, "we may need it!"

"I did bring one, Kenny," responded Karin.

"Wonderful! You're an efficient secretary!" he replied, giving her a quick hug.

Alyssia, Sarah and the space beings had gathered around by then, so Viridiana escorted them all to a building that stood in a courtyard, but it was not like the ones on Earth. This one was full of creeping vines, large bushes with bright flowers on, a stream that ran through it, masses of butterflies and green lizards, as well as green birds the size of pigeons that gently warbled to each other in a fairly high-toned melody. To cap it all, there were fruits growing at the same time as the flowers, and the group noticed they were ripening continuously while they were walking past.

The door to the building was wooden, and even that, like the wooden building, had a green tinged sheen to it. The building had an archaic look to it, with rounded windows, and it looked as if it had been standing for centuries, for also here and there, there were fragrantly perfumed climbing plants adorning its walls.
"What a beautiful building!" exclaimed Alyssia.
"Artists always appreciate things well!" responded Viridiana.
"It looks so familiar," said Kenny to Karin, and she nodded.
"It will become even more so once inside, my friends," responded Viridiana.

Chapter 8– Behind Closed Doors

Inside the building, the light was muted and dappled, with the many trees by the building, and the many creepers and vines on the outer walls. An old staircase took them to the first floor. Beside the base of the staircase, a long corridor led to a number of rooms on the ground floor. Viridiana escorted them all into a large sunny room with a veranda.
"Take a seat on the veranda, everyone! I shall be back shortly!" she announced.
Alyssia and Sarah led the way, followed closely by Karin and Kenny, and then Zanadar, Siral, Salaron and Maeron.
"We will leave you shortly, my friends!" said Zanadar, "but don't worry," he responded, when he saw the look of surprise on the group's faces, "we won't be gone for long, and we'll know when you will have completed your journey here."
"We have a small job to do, as we have been called to assist, you see!" explained Siral.
"…And we will return very soon, in time for your need to visit Astragandara!" added Salaron.
"Can we ask what job you have to do?" enquired Kenny.
"We are going to help give advice to others of our kind, who are on their first mission. We hoped it would have been later on, but they need to set off very soon, therefore we are obliged to give them some timely advice," explained Siral.

Viridiana returned with some drinks on a tray, except that the tray was floating along in front of her, and she had some objects in her arms. She concentrated on the tray as she came to the veranda, and it gently lowered itself onto a table in front of them all, amid appreciative murmurs.
"Help yourself to a glass of essence and some fruit," said Viridiana.
"It's just like the essence in the Garden of Eden!" exclaimed Alyssia.
Viridiana smiled broadly, "we do have our own equivalent here too, you know, all good planets do!"
Sarah looked thoughtful for a moment, and then uttered, "the essence has come from a very beautiful well in a bright green glade."
"That's right!" said Karin, "it's such a potent place, like the Garden of Eden on Earth, I can feel the strength of the place, and it holds deep pools of bright green waters."
Karin's face looked serious and intent a moment.

"The souls of those who would attune to our waters are welcome to approach. Seek the deep wisdom to be found at our abode, blessed be." Karin smiled a moment, "that was channelled from one of the well spirits."
"Your first channelled message, Karin, that's lovely!" cried Sarah.
"Viridiana, will we be able to visit your Garden of Eden?" asked Kenny, and he exchanged a warm glance with Karin.
"It's a certainty!" smiled Viridiana, "and one of the main reasons for coming here, but first, I intend to show you around this building."
"So we can re-acquaint ourselves with our native planet," commented Karin, and Kenny and Viridiana smiled knowingly.
"It has been a great pleasure to re-visit Verdamara again, however, I sense we ought to leave now," said Siral, smiling kindly.
"He's right! A message is coming up that we need to reach the nearest starway quite soon, so we can be intercepted by the mission craft, and then we can travel together," explained Zanadar.
"I know you are wondering where we are heading towards! However, we are not allowed to give any details away, but it is in the adjacent universe, so it is of no concern to you all," commented Salaron, considerately.
"Let us depart, all!" announced Zanadar, and he held up his hand in the usual salute to those remaining, who responded accordingly. The other space beings also joined in.
Viridiana rose to escort them out of the building.
"Do not trouble yourself, Viridiana. We will find our own way back to the spaceship," Zanadar insisted, kindly.
The space beings left with a wave. Viridiana and the group looked over the veranda, and gave them all another good wave, until they became obscured by greenery.
"If you would like any more essence water before we begin to explore the building, please help yourselves," announced Viridiana.
"There isn't much left though, Viridiana," exclaimed Alyssia, glancing at the nearly empty jug, and then at Viridiana.
"Oh! Verdantia!" cried Viridiana loudly.
There was a flash of green, with a broad smile somewhere within it, and in its wake, another full jug of essence spring water emerged.
Once everyone had realised that the water jug was real and not an apparition, they poured its contents into their glasses, and had a good long drink. Viridiana encouraged them to top up

again, and take the glasses with them as they moved around the building. They followed Viridiana back downstairs and along the corridor to the furthest door. It was quite an unobtrusive door. As they approached it, Viridiana sang some notes gently.
"I feel rather strange," said Kenny, looking at Karin.
Karin then turned to look at Kenny, "I feel a bit odd myself."
"Look at that door!" said Alyssia, in a half whisper.
The door had now become eloquently carved with animal shapes all over it, their eyes looking out at them. The daylight was muted in that area.
"They are all beginning to move!" cried Sarah.
"Where's Viridiana!" said Kenny, "she seems to have gone!"
Karin and Sarah looked all around and shrugged their shoulders.
"I'm here!" indicated a voice.
"Who's that?" asked Kenny, "and where are you?"
"Viridiana, and I'm on the door!" she said.
The group all exchanged puzzled glances, but looked at the door anyway.
"There! Behind that lizard's face!" cried Alyssia.
"Viridiana, why are you there?" asked Kenny.
Viridiana looked as if she was pointing to something in front of her, then she looked at the group.
"You each have one!" she exclaimed.
She was pointing to something in front of her, that she appeared to be holding in her hand," commented Sarah, "and that could only be a crystal!"
Everyone reached into their bags, but with the strange atmosphere, it took longer to find their crystals. They each brought them out, and pointed them at the door, looking at Viridiana.
"Chant!" said Viridiana.
"Halu-maiyee, kalukah-ayee, keralah-daya, melarana-ayee," said Kenny and Karin, from somewhere within themselves.
A bright viridian light spun around them all, and then they were inside the room behind that door, and there was Viridiana.
"Remember, remember!" emphasised Viridiana, "it's very important, will this help?"
She drew out her own crystal and concentrated hard in front of her. The room faded gradually, and the sound of a tiny stream was audible, and also the soughing of a gentle breeze through a canopy of leaves. Then everyone could discern that they were in a forest with a peaty soil below them, the leaves bright green. Viridiana indicated for them to follow. The little stream was with them all the way. By a tree root there was a little door. As they approached, the door expanded and they all entered, walking

down a winding staircase below ground. After what seemed like half an hour, they came to another door.

"Just touch it with your crystal wands," advised Viridiana.

They did so, and the door became transparent and barely tangible. They could see what lay beyond, a mass of crystals and glistening rocks.

"Lie down here!" instructed Viridiana, "and close your eyes!"

They could feel the crystals converging around them, and they felt surrounded by their love and peace.

Karin could see herself with green limbs, moving down through time, sitting beside friends in the glades, worshipping in ancient temples with the roof always open to the skies or canopy above, listening to wise people, taking to the skies to visit Reluisia and other nearby planets, talking to the earth spirits, the trees and the various animals and birds native to Verdamara.

"It is as if I've never left, my home!" thought Karin.

Kenny could see the spirits inside the crystals, and he greeted them, and they all exuded a loving response. Now he could see many Verdamaran people, and he saw his own reflection in a nearby pool, and its reflection was the same green. He could see himself being ushered somewhere, and he found himself in front of an expectant audience, and then he was speaking. He could see himself turning to the wall behind himself, and there were charts.

'What were they of?' thought Kenny, and he tried to pinpoint them, but the more he tried, the less they revealed themselves.

'Perhaps if I don't take so much notice, they may reveal their secrets!' and so he just prayed they would.

Alyssia saw the deep pools and wells, and that beautiful shimmering water with shoals of turquoise-green fish gliding around. The green glades reflected on the water's surface, emphasised that beauty of the greenery, as well as the multicoloured array of blossoms, in hues of pink, red, peach, cream and deep yellow. At certain times, Alyssia intuited, the blossoms would fall onto the water's surface, forming a petal carpet of bright colours, which would look incongruous on a green planet!

Sarah could see many waterfalls cascading in abundance, some long and thin, and others of spectacular size, with masses of water thundering over high cliffs. The rocks nearby were coated with damp-loving, bright green mosses. 'Just the sort of places for a herb healing person like me, I hope I'll see some like this on Astragandara as well!'

Once their visions faded, they found themselves back in the room again. After exchanging their visions for a short while, they made ready to move on.

"We are going into the next room now!" announced Viridiana. Within a few seconds, the humble door frame became an arched one with a filigree of lattice work in wood, all within the door frame itself.

"What an intricately carved door," cried Karin, "I can see all kinds of birds in it."

"There are berries and flowers too, as well as herbs," said Sarah.

"I can see elves and gnomes; I can't see any berries, birds or flowers," countered Kenny.

"I can see a symbol right in the middle, here," pointed Alyssia, and a rather perplexed group of eyes focused where Alyssia indicated, and then they looked at Alyssia questioningly. Finally, they all looked at Viridiana.

"Yes, you are all seeing different things, and they are all valid because they are all contained within nature's spirit, and so are symbols." Viridiana then looked at Alyssia directly. "Tell us about this symbol you saw, Alyssia."

"It was a circular shape, and within that circle were two triangles on top of each other. The top one was pointing upwards, and the other one was pointing downwards, so it looked like an octahedron, but I could tell the triangles were independent from one another, as they moved in different directions. A shaft of light emanated from each of the sides of the upper triangle, and I saw an aperture in the lower triangle out of which a rainbow-like arc stretched to the sides of the circle. That sums it up; what does it mean, Viridiana?" queried Alyssia.

"Viridiana looked thoughtful, "it is an old symbol, going back to the origins of this planet. The triangles are three sided pyramids and are used by gnomes and other planetary spirits to generate a certain type of energy. The upright pyramid is used to generate the path towards bringing in energy from the heavens, as given by the shafts of light. The inverted pyramid is of the gnomes, who bring up planetary energy, but they also intercept energy brought downwards, and so they use it as well as the other type. Out of all this, the rainbow energy denotes the great harmony achieved, and how it maintains the good frequency of our planet. You did well to see it, not everyone on our planet has managed, so it is impressive that a visitor has done so!"

"Is this room linked to the origins of this planet, like Akashic records, and the energy frequency of it?" asked Karin.

"Yes, you are right!" cried Viridiana, "spot on, as your people might say!"

Here, she paused to formulate her next thoughts into words.

"In the beginning, the planet was populated from worlds at the very centre of our universe, as our neighbouring planets were. So we brought the first blueprints of codes and ways of living onto the planet with us, knowing that we then would have to adapt to the nature of the planet as we continued to live on Verdamara, as well as our own natures. As we progressed, our own sense of perspective altered gradually, as our perception of spiritual growth progressed, and so, many constructive additions to our understanding took place. We are lucky in that we hold our own records of life on Verdamara from the beginning. In your case, your planet has been constantly besieged by many disruptions, so there are too many obstacles to keep the spiritual understanding flowing constantly, very hard for you!"

"Is there any way to gain access to our own Akashic record in entirety?" asked Sarah.

"It must be possible I would have thought, since on our planet, almost every other kind of information is so well documented and duplicated many times over!" commented Kenny.

Viridiana smiled, "yes we know about your electronic systems that leak information very easily! As for the Akashic system, yes there are records held in other places, which can be tapped into if it is allowed, but not easy to consider writing about all the information on your planet. It would be an enormous task for many scores of people to consider."

"I suppose all that is required and useful to be known, will filter through to appropriate people," said Karin.

"Well said, and that will be sufficient!" concluded Viridiana.

They all found themselves back in the corridor, and Viridiana ushered everyone outside into the sunny courtyard.

"Think of the Garden of Eden, and ours is called Verdantia!" announced Viridiana.

They stood in a circle together and concentrated. There was a shimmering of light, the surroundings were blurred, and then they found themselves in a forest.

"A much quicker way to travel than all those vehicles you have on your planet!" smiled Viridiana. "Now, we are in the forest that leads up to Verdantia. We just follow this path, and we will soon be there."

After a short while of walking, the group began to notice the changes as they approached their destination.

"The foliage looks even greener! I didn't think it could have been possible, since it's so splendid already!" exclaimed Sarah.

"The birdsong gets better and more varied with every few steps we take!" said Alyssia, with an inspired look.
"I can hear something," commented Karin, "like faint murmuring of prayers all the time."
"I've seen lots of elves and gnomes, like they've been hinting of their presence very fleetingly, without being intercepted by anyone else," commented Kenny.
"We are coming to the boundary point now, everyone, and you will notice more changes from now on," said Viridiana.

As they continued, they began to hear the sound of water in the background to the abundant birdsong. The gnomes and elves Kenny intercepted became very visible and smiled over to the group, while they were busy tending to plants and earth energies.
The path began to lead downwards, and wound its way increasingly, the steeper the slope became.
"How many waterfalls and cascades are there leading into this valley, Viridiana?" exclaimed Alyssia in amazement at the dramatic vista in front of them, seen through a clearing amongst the luxuriant foliage.
"Incredibly, there are seven waterfalls!" cried Viridiana.
"Hasn't your Eden temple been washed away yet, with all that water?" queried Kenny with a humorous glint in his eyes.
Viridiana laughed, "no! The Temple and the Garden are situated on ground that is a bit higher than the watery base of those falls."
"How do we get to the Garden?" asked Sarah, who looked anxious, remembering their last leap over the chasm to the cave.
"We can levitate, but we can't claim to enjoy it very much, Viridiana!" responded Kenny.
"There is a land bridge, my friends!" smiled Viridiana.

They ventured further, and the sound of water became louder. Viridiana turned to speak to everyone.
"Soon we won't be able to hear one another, so I shall tell you where we're going now," explained Viridiana. "We shall descend a bit more, and we will come to the land bridge. We go over it and the temple lies on the other side. Take care on the bridge, as the watery mist makes the ground very wet, and may be slippery. Once on the other side, just follow me to the temple. We shall have some company too, as well as other nature spirits we have seen of their kind already."

Soon enough, the land bridge was in front of them. It was about six feet wide on average, and in places, the mist became quite dense. They all proceeded slowly across. Sarah was looking at the plants growing there, and enthused about the spangly, pale mauve and blue flowered plants growing either side of them.

They huddled together so as to guarantee no one would get lost in the thick of the mist. The land bridge began to descend a little. Viridiana turned to caution them all as they were approaching some stone steps. Once down them, there was a huge amount of greenery again, which insulated them a little from the pervasive sound of the surging waters. The temple area was situated within a hollow area of lower ground in the centre of the trees.

Viridiana took them near the temple door, and indicated for them to sit nearby in a glady area. The group began to notice moss covered standing stones surrounding them against the trees. Each of them went to a stone and sat beside it without need of discussion, and slipped into a meditative state.

"Welcome to our world, my friends!" came a strong voice to everyone in the Oswestry group.

The mists seemed to clear a little, for the group began to feel the warmth of the sun to a small degree. Suddenly, everyone was aware of a brilliant flash of light, and a sensation of tumbling off the planet into the centre of brilliant sunlight, with myriad beings around them, with very kind eyes emanating strong love towards them.

"This place is linked to the centre of the planet and to no-time, that is why you have lifted into a non-material level unlinked to any given planet," said the voice again.

Everyone tried to look inwardly to the direction of that voice, but the light stopped them from seeing anyone.

"The Garden of Eden on Earth is so different from this one," said Alyssia.

"Is the Garden of Eden to be experienced from this circle?" asked Karin.

"Just partly, this Garden of Eden is different due to its being in a higher dimensional region, therefore we can link higher than on your planet, and so there is less pull on being planet-bound, as you can see! We are going no-where in particular, though that may confuse people from three-dimensional worlds!"

"Are we just staying in the same place?" asked Sarah.

"In a way, yes, but will have lessened the density, and so a different vista presents itself to us all. See what you can find, my friends!" explained the voice.

"By the way, who are you, please?" asked Kenny.

"I am one of the Eden Guardians, and also a holder of the light of the Source, my name is Arala Suriya, blessed be."

With that, a pale sea green clothed female figure momentarily came into view, and then faded again.

Chapter 9 – The Shining Presences

Everyone came out of meditation and looked around at each other.
"So the Garden of Eden is in a different dimension?" asked Alyssia, "will we have to meditate to link to it?"
"Just sit here for a little while to become acclimatised," answered Viridiana, "remember you are on a fifth dimensional planet, therefore you are doing well already. The Garden of Eden is of sixth dimensional capacity, but can be appreciated at the higher end of the fifth dimensional spectrum."
"Yes, it is a joy to be part of the fifth dimension here," said Sarah, "It's just so peaceful and joyous!"
"I keep wanting to dance and sing!" cried Karin.
"Don't let anything stop you!" replied Kenny, with a smile.
"I think I need some practice first!" responded Karin.
"You'll get that for sure, soon enough!" said Viridiana, with a knowing smile, and everyone looked at her, intrigued.
Viridiana signalled for them to get up, after a short while, and so they arose and slowly looked around themselves.
"I can see sparkling light everywhere!" exclaimed Alyssia.
"Yes, you're right!" agreed Sarah.
"Although we were more aware of the energy around everything on this planet, I realise there's much more to be revealed," commented Karin.
They all marvelled at the myriad of nature spirits who had become entirely visible, and they could hear them all singing gently as they worked, and were at a higher frequency than Earth. Viridiana beckoned the group to the gates of the Garden of Eden, and as they entered, the sounds of the trees, flowers and rocks became apparent, and despite the diversity, there was still great harmony. Then they were aware of other notes from the rocks deeper in the ground inside the planet herself.
"If you were on planet Earth and seeing with fifth and sixth dimensional eyes, you would be aware of all the disharmonious energy down the ages that hadn't been resolved. Whereas here, all is well and you can focus on that instead!" explained Viridiana.
"Surely there are some good places on Earth where you'd be focusing on good energy?" asked Alyssia.
"Yes, I know there are truly, but it is surrounded by unresolved energy that needs to be changed before the whole can reach the level of our planet. That's what I mean," replied Viridiana, smiling gently.

"I see what you mean," responded Alyssia, "it's never going to be at its best unless the rest is sorted out."
"But of course these places are oases and very necessary, so keep working on producing them," replied Viridiana.

A pathway amongst the trees wound through the most luxuriant foliage and flora the group had ever seen. They all stopped, looking around with expressions of amazed joy.
"Look at that! It's all spangly and radiating light!" cried Sarah, "and it's singing too!" and she touched a huge rose-like flower gently, and it emanated a fragrant perfume while the notes seemed to flow straight to her.
Sarah looked very moved, and then became quite trance-like. The others became trance-like also, affected by the fragrances and the melody. Viridiana had to keep on encouraging them all to keep moving onwards until they reached the temple antechamber.
"Now, I think it is time you rested a little after that perfume!" said Viridiana, decisively.
"I do feel very sleepy," agreed Kenny, who was just awake enough to speak, but the words were very slowly pronounced.
"It all seems far too wonderful here just to sleep!" commented Sarah.
Having heard Kenny, she used all her strength to utter her words.
"I know, but it is necessary, and won't be for very long," replied Viridiana.
There were some relaxing seats for everyone, who, once seated, were soon fast asleep.

Viridiana turned her attention skyward, and appeared to be communicating with various beings. After half an hour by Earth timescale, she looked towards a group of elemental beings who came over, and showered the slumbering group with a sparkling, translucent white powder, and everyone began to stir. The group looked around and saw the elemental beings beside Viridiana.
"Hello! Have we been asleep for long?" asked Sarah.
"Not as long as Rip Van Winkle!" replied one elemental.
Kenny chuckled, "that's all right then!"
"Look at this powder! Where has it come from?" asked Alyssia.
"Is it from the essence of the Garden of Eden?" asked Karin.
Kenny looked at it for a moment in thought, then to the elementals.

"I think these fellows spread it over us to make us awaken!" he stated decisively.
"Correct, my friend!" cried another elemental.

The group arose to continue inside the temple, and said goodbye to the elementals. The passageway became like moving through the entrance to a cave, or like into a burial chamber or fogou, as Alyssia mentioned afterwards. The ground rose a little for a while, and then a little more. By now the passage was very dark, and was lit periodically by candles, so it seemed, later found out to be concentrated points of energy held there by the spirits of the place. Eventually, the group found themselves at an area of pathway where it rose sharply and climbing was needed. Viridiana chanted a word a few times, and steps became visible amid the earthy brown light. Ascending for a few minutes, light began to shine into the passageway, and then the whole passage opened out and they were outside on open ground and daylight once more.
"It almost feels strange to be outside again!" cried Sarah.
They looked out, but were surrounded by a mass of cloud, all sparkling in the sunlight.
"Are we really so high up?" asked Alyssia.
"I can't hear any waterfalls!" exclaimed Karin.
"Where on Verdamara are we?" enquired Kenny.
"Please sit down a moment and I will explain," instructed Viridiana.
Everyone noticed a ledge around the perimeter and they sat down, periodically peering over the edge into the clouds.
"It's a bit like Anchorin's temple clouds!" said Sarah.
Viridiana smiled and nodded, and she paused for thought.
"I wish to tell you that your journey through the tunnel, or cavern route as we call it, has given you all special energies for what we shall do next. There is no cause for concern, but I am going to take you upwards from this point, and we will walk up this spiral staircase just here," explained Viridiana, pointing in front of her, and in the centre of them all.
Of course, the spiral staircase wasn't visible to anyone, and so everyone's faces looked understandably worried. Viridiana stood up. "Now! Everyone stand up and do as I do, and you will be perfectly safe. You will not see a sea of cloud for much longer, nor a cliff edge or dizzying view down to the ground. Just forget about that and concentrate only on these steps. Come behind me and just follow, and focus on that. Nothing else!"
Viridiana looked at everyone emphatically, and the group acknowledged her words by nods and assents.

She began by taking two steps, and she ushered Sarah to follow. Sarah took a step, then exclaimed.
"You can see the steps once you step on them!"
They all began their slow climb heavenwards. The group focused only on the steps. Then Viridiana spoke.
"We are almost up to the top!" she announced happily.
As they all reached the top, a vista awaited them.

It was a landscape of light. There were temples encircling them, and a larger one in the centre. All was very bright for the first few minutes, and then all began to appear in more natural colours, with that verdant greenery in abundance. They all walked to the central temple and went indoors. There were three female Guardians sat by the altar, and looked as if they were in deep meditation. Viridiana beckoned for the group to sit on some benches in front of these beings. Slowly the beings' eyes opened, and the group saw how bright their eyes were, as if illumined from the inside. Then a radiance was perceivable, emanating from within them. The radiance filled the whole temple and began to seep into the group's auras.
'It's like I know the underlying purpose behind what is happening on Verdamara, Reluisia and other neighbouring planets, the next rung in their evolvement,' thought Alyssia.
'I can feel what all the elementals know about life on this planet, and others nearby,' thought Kenny.
'I can hear words echoing from all time periods, and now I've been told I can choose what to hear, when I wish,' thought Karin.
'It is as if I know exactly where to find herbs on Verdamara, and just walk to them easily. I can also see where the herbs are obtainable on other planets too, how amazing!' thought Sarah.
The energy kept coming from the beings until all of them found it was all too much and gently became unconscious. Then they awoke soon afterwards to find themselves slumped forwards, and the three beings looked over compassionately. As they sent these thoughts, the group instantly understood of their caring energy, and that the group knew what they needed to know from Verdamara, and that the Council of Twelve spaceship would collect the group very soon.

The group profusely thanked the Garden of Eden Guardians and then returned the way they came. They followed Viridiana down the spiral staircase and along the cavern route, and then back to the entrance near the standing stones and the sound of cascading water. Viridiana then meditated with the group to transport themselves back to the building, where Zanadar and the others were waiting.

"It is time to visit Astragandara now!" he said.

Zanadar viewed the group's faces, although happy and excited, they looked tired, "don't worry, you can rest while we travel, my friends!" he said.

"It is wonderfully exciting, but I do need to pace myself, just a little!" cried Sarah, chuckling.

They all thanked Viridiana enthusiastically, and then set off on the spaceship.

After a tired but excited initial discussion of what had happened on the planet, Zanadar insisted the group all get some rest. They were profoundly relieved to lie down and sleep. Siral and Maeron had thoughtfully left some of the rejuvenating drink for them all to have, at any time, while in their rooms.

"Let's have some now, and then more when we wake up!" said Alyssia.

"I'll go with that!" replied Sarah.

They had a glassful and settled down to sleep.

Meanwhile, Zanadar at the helm was guiding the spaceship onwards. Siral and Maeron were beside him. Aurion, Salaron and Golan were checking the ship over.

"It won't be long before we'll arrive at Astragandara, will it?" asked Siral.

"No, merely a couple of hours by Earth time, but it should give them enough time to recuperate, then escort them down," replied Zanadar.

"It is an impressive planet to look at, so let's all make a point of viewing it!" responded Maeron.

"Yes indeed! That would be excellent. I shall inform everyone when the time approaches!" replied Zanadar, with an animated smile, and he turned again to look at his controls and also at the vista of pale green light.

The others stood beside him and they all adopted an expression of deep concentration, periodically nodding or other slight facial gestures, for they were communing with other beings from planets that the ship was passing. They were checking up on how things are, but also linking with good friends, and those from their own planets who visit other ones to aid interplanetary culture, and Zanadar's ship also often carried people around for this purpose.

With that, three graceful beings dressed in pink, with a pearly pink skin, came into the control room from the guest quarters.

"Greetings to you all!" cried Zanadar, while Siral and Maeron bowed graciously, and they smiled cheerfully.

"Hello Galayah, Enalda and Siraldah. The Earth people are on board looking forward to visiting Astragandara also," commented Siral.

"They will be pleasantly surprised to know you are all on board!" said Maeron.

"It is quite some time since we've visited Astragandara, but we can contact them by thought, so we keep in touch. It is certainly a lovely planet to visit," said Galayah.

"Your planet is very beautiful indeed! Though I was keen to return to my native planet region, I certainly missed all those pink flowers and foliage, and as for those sunsets! Spectacular!" responded Siral.

"Let's say it's lovely to have so much beauty to choose from all planets in our universe!" stated Siraldah, emphatically.

"We all agree with that!" they all said in unison, and began laughing happily.

Aurion, Salaron and Golan returned from their maintenance-checking shift, and could intuit what they were laughing about, and smiled in response.

"We only have a small amount of work to do on the ship, and for the final touch, a top up of that Astragandaran substance is required!" implied Aurion.

"It is most useful, invaluable in fact," said Golan in agreement.

"What is this substance, and what does it do?" asked Enalda.

"It acts as a catalyst, in helping to alter the frequency levels of the spaceship, depending in which dimension or universe we are visiting. This substance travels throughout all the ship's structure via ducts. It looks a little like liquid crystal, mixed with energy from the core of the sun, and we call it zircona-solar-viridium. That name covers some of its aspects, but there are many other parts to it, though a very long name is not convenient enough to say!" explained Salaron.

"You mean the Central Spiritual Sun?" asked Siraldah.

"Yes indeed!" replied Salaron.

Then there were sounds emanating from down the corridor, and the Oswestry group began to appear. Alyssia and Karin were the first to emerge.

"Greetings to the two of you!" cried Zanadar, "are the other two nearly ready?"

"They shall be along very soon," replied Alyssia.

"You see, there will be the view of the approach to Astragandara coming up quite soon, just tell your friends it will happen in

twenty minutes time. There's some food to hand in that cupboard and hatch area," said Zanadar, indicating where they should look.
So Sarah and Alyssia sent a telepathic message to the others.
As Alyssia and Karin were gathering food, Kenny and Sarah came through and joined the other two for breakfast. As they settled down to eat, they realised the presence of the three Reluisian females, and waved to them, and the Reluisians waved back.

Then the moment occurred on screen, when Astragandara became visible. There were slight gasps of amazement from the Oswestry group as the bright sphere of pale golden hue came into view, emanating frequent showers of pale golden light, which cascaded over the surface of the planet. A bright rainbow-like arc of energy from further in towards the centre of the universe began to radiate light over towards Astragandara, illuminating it from behind, so that there was a slight silhouette, with a brilliant, silver lining all around, and silhouettes of the emanating showers of light from the planet periodically.
"What an intriguing planet!" stated Alyssia.
"I can't wait to see what herbs there are!" cried Sarah.
Everyone smiled at one another with enthusiasm, and felt a glow in their hearts that became increasingly potent.
Zanadar looked around at everyone in that state.
"Astragandara always affects everyone like this, it has so much peace, love and beauty, that it simply overflows!"
Now it looked as if everyone had gone into a deeply meditative state, with this love emanating in their direction, their expressions of reverie held sway, but they acknowledged Zanadar's comment with a slight nod and a smile.
Zanadar smiled in response, knowingly.

Astragandara drew nearer, and everyone was still held spellbound, looking at all the lustrous gold showers within the luminous energy sparkling around the planet.
"I don't like to break the meditative state for everyone, but it is time to go to the disembarkation chamber now, as we are about to land!" announced Zanadar quite loudly.
Everyone made an effort to divert their attention from the screen, and began walking towards the corridor that led to the antechamber of the disembarkation platform. Meanwhile, they were aware of the ship's landing and engine cut out, and then Golan duly mustered everyone to be in place on the platform, including Zanadar, Aurion and Salaron, which was lowered to the

ground, and they all took their first step onto Astragandaran soil.

"You know, this planet is the closest one to the sixth dimension, in fact it is able to encompass it!" said Alyssia, looking at Zanadar.

"Indeed! You should know, being a native!" he responded.

The memories of their time in Lemuria on the crystal mountain flashed back to Alyssia and Sarah. There was a musical humming sound, slightly muffled.

"Ah! The Glorae-astraespheres are coming to life, Sarah!" cried Alyssia.

"Let's get them out then!" responded Sarah.

As soon as they both opened their bags, the Glorae-astraespheres hummed even more strongly, began to hover above Sarah's and Alyssia's hands, and then shot off, to their amazement.

"Where on earth have they gone?" cried Alyssia, with a look of disappointment.

There was a burst of gentle light, and three angelic beings appeared beside them all.

"Welcome, Valana and Salana! Welcome all!" they said to the visitors, "come, we have some food awaiting your arrival."

The angelic beings turned to Alyssia and Sarah, "do not be concerned about your Glorae-astraespheres, they always do that if returning to Astragandara, as they are replenishing their energy and meeting with others of their kind, as well as linking to the planet itself. They'll return in due course, you'll see!"

"That's a relief," responded Sarah, and Alyssia agreed.

They were both looking around for the golden iridescent flowers they had seen in their meditation.

"Can you hear that faint music, Sarah?" asked Alyssia.

"Yes, it's not the Glorae-astraespheres, but flowers I think, possibly those rose-like ones," responded Sarah.

The whole group rounded a corner on the way to the dining establishment, and saw the building concerned. It was of a golden hue and dome shaped, with arch shaped doors and windows. Just in front of the building was a mass of flowers.

"There they are!" cried Sarah.

The Oswestry group all moved swiftly over to examine the rose-like flowers. The melody was elusive and beautiful, harking back to ancient times on Earth when all was pristine.

"That perfume is very powerful," said Sarah, "I feel something profound is going on just by smelling it."

"Too right!" agreed Karin, "it's as moving as our time in the Earth's Garden of Eden and the cave."

"I've not seen any native spirits yet," commented Kenny.
The flowers suddenly became very sparkly, and the perfume became even more powerful. It was a very perfume-intoxicated group that entered the dining area. The three angels guided the group to their seats.
"Drink this, it will help your condition," said one of them.
It was that effervescent drink the group knew so well, and they looked at each other knowingly.

The food was anticipated by the group, and Kenny looked around expectantly. Suddenly, a plate with some sparkling gold leaves appeared in front of Kenny.
"Are they ornaments?" he asked, and everyone laughed. The three angels smiled.
"The leaves are food, we thought you'd enjoy them!"
"Well!" ventured Kenny, "they're very artistic."
A bowl then appeared in front of him with a golden liquid in it. Kenny looked down and gave a small 'oh'. Everyone began laughing again.
"This is the type of food we usually have available on Astragandara, you know!" responded the angels, but we, ourselves, don't need to eat or drink!"
Then dishes of vegetables, fruits and nuts appeared amongst the group, and Kenny looked happier.

The angels were all much the same in appearance to the group, about fifteen feet high, with a lot of white and golden light around themselves, and those vibrant emanations that appear to be like wings. They showed faces to the group, as well as a kind of body, but their natural state from the fifth dimension onwards was like a shaft of light, with those emanations radiating from them.
"We ought to introduce ourselves really, though in reality, names and identities are not important, for we all work together as one," explained one angel.
"Yes, we can appreciate that," replied Sarah.
"My name is Aurial," said one.
"...and my name is Astara," said the second.
"...and my name is Aurastara," said the third, "and it just denotes our work or origins."
The only problem is that you all look so alike, so we won't know who is who!" said Kenny, "how will we know?"
"You will feel the effects of our different energy fields through your feet," explained Aurial, "we will show you after the meal."

Once outside again, the three angels took the group over to a grassy area.

"Even the grass has a translucent, sparkly gold look to it!" cried Kenny.

"Now everyone, take off your shoes and I will transmit my energy towards you!" announced Aurial.

They did so, and stood there in anticipation.

Aurial concentrated, and after a few minutes, asked everyone for their comments.

"It is a bright, smooth kind of energy, like a shaft of sunlight," said Sarah.

"I could see golden light streaming," said Alyssia.

"I could hear a sound of voices singing a note," said Karin.

Everyone looked at Kenny.

"I just got a feeling of movement and joyful energy," he said.

"That is very fitting, and it is good that you all perceive different aspects of vibrational energy," said Aurial.

Astara then stepped forward, looked at the group and smiled, indicating for them to try again. After a short while, the group began to explain what they perceived.

"The energy was stronger and more strident somehow," explained Kenny, "I'm not sure strident is the best word, not smooth and unchangeable like Aurial, anyway."

"I could hear many notes repeated several times, but sometimes they were loud, others softer, but quickly," said Karin.

"It is like a series of bursts of sunlight, some stronger than others and quite rapid, like a flickering motion," explained Sarah.

"I could see the flickering light flashing brightly and rapidly, and happens because you receive heavenly light and send it out very quickly," said Alyssia.

"Very interesting responses, everyone! Now you know my energy field," replied Astara. "In a way, my energy could have streamed in constantly like Aurial's, but Aurial's energy comes from the Source directly, where the energy is masculine, but mine comes from the feminine part of the Source, where the light is a bit softer and pearly, and does flicker as well."

Astara moved to one side, and Aurastara approached.

"You can try my energy now!" said Aurastara.

After a minute everyone stopped concentrating.

"The energy felt very gentle and flowing," said Kenny.

"I could see it like in gentle waves that swirled around, no straight movement at all," explained Alyssia.

"The notes sounded like a collection of rhythms that came and went," said Karin.

"The energy was soothing, like a trickling stream, very relaxing in fact!" finalised Sarah.

"You are all correct, my friends," replied Aurastara, "and now you know our energy fields and who we are. By the way, I am from the feminine aspect of the Source as well. Though it may be a challenge for you to know and remember two hundred or more energy fields!"

"It certainly would!" responded Kenny, smiling broadly.

"Don't worry, it is a knack that can be learnt in time," replied Aurastara.

"You know, we've been so occupied, I hadn't noticed that Zanadar and the others aren't still with us!" cried Alyssia.

"Yes, they slipped away quite soundlessly!" agreed Karin.

"It is all right," explained Aurial, "some of the others knew about Zanadar's wish to refill his ship with the trans-dimensional liquid, so he and his crew became occupied. We'll see them again, shortly."

"Yes," said Astara, "we are all going to visit a special place," and she gave a knowing look, "any guesses as to where it might be?"

"Another Garden of Eden, I think!" remarked Kenny.

"Correct!" replied Astara, "we will leave very soon to visit, and the others will approach just in time!"

They all enjoyed a while, being taken around the herbal gardens in the area.

"This is amazing!" exclaimed Sarah animatedly, "so the origins of all medical herbs begins here, on Astragandara!"

"Indeed it does!" replied Aurial, "and is easily exported to other planets via the space ships, and from any time period to any time period!"

"Absolutely splendid!" cried Sarah, examining a gold-tinged filigree leaf; "in both cases!" she smiled.

"That is now a Reluisian herb," explained Astara, "it was originally golden on Astragandara, as you see it now, but became a deep pink with gold flecks when on Reluisia."

"What is its function?" asked Sarah.

"It is deeply healing, and also helps if people travel a lot, moving from one dimension to another in quick succession, and the usual methods are not working as well, explained Astara, "it's basically a very efficient pick-me-up."

At that moment, the four Reluisian beings came walking past.

"Oh, what a lovely herb it is! I thought I recognised it," remarked Leana.

"It's called a spanglelace plant," said Galaya.

At the name being mentioned, the Oswestry group let out an exclamation.

"What are the flowers by the dining hall called?" asked Sarah.

"Spanglefoil, since they are all metallic silvers and golds," explained Galaya.

"We are off! Just touring around the area for a short while," remarked Leana.

"…For a few days until the next space ship visits, and then we shall return to Reluisia!" commented Siraldah.

"Goodbye!" said the Reluisians in unison.

"Goodbye!" everyone replied.

"Perhaps we may see you again on a space ship?" said the Oswestry group.

"Hello!" said Zanadar, Aurion and Salaron. They laughed jovially at surprising everyone.

"We didn't mean to startle you!" responded Aurion, "you were focused on your Reluisian friends."

"I suppose we weren't expecting you back so promptly," remarked Astara, "at least, not for another hour or so."

"Yes, things were achieved quicker than expected," replied Aurion, "we have the ship all sorted out now."

"We are leaving for the Astragandaran version of the Garden of Eden, any time now!" said Aurial.

"Is everyone ready?" enquired Astara.

Then you can all take some of this plant mix," said Aurastara, "just help yourselves to a small amount, like this!" and she showed a small ball of herbs sitting in the very centre of her palm, "and then chew it!"

She then held out a bag of it, for people to take the herb amounts from it.

Sarah was examining the bag too, which was silver, with small golden flecks through it, which seemed filled with light.

"Does this material help to maintain the quality of the herbs?" asked Sarah.

"Indeed it does, can't you recall carrying a bag around with you wherever you went?" asked Aurial, "have a closer look again."

Sarah examined the bag again, and her face became impassive, as she focused within for a while, and then returned to a state of alertness.

"I do recall! I could see myself carrying my bag, and collecting herbs, getting to know new ways of applying the herbs, to benefit less advanced planets," explained Sarah, looking moved and thoughtful.

"What does this herb do?" asked Kenny.

"It raises your level of awareness!" said Aurastara.

"And also helps you to fly!" commented Aurial, and she rose upwards about six feet, hovering above the group.

"Let's go!" cried Aurastara, indicating for everyone to rise upwards, which they did with ease.

They all flew off, away from the direction of the eating hall, towards some rolling hills. As they rose higher to clear the tops of trees, they could look down on leaves that were burnished with various shades of gold, copper and silver. A range of mountains became apparent on the horizon.

"We are making for those mountains, as the Garden of Eden lies near them," explained Astara.

Chapter 10 – The Garden of Astragandara

The burnished foliage glinted and sparkled beneath them, as they flew onwards. Here and there, small pools of water, like tarns, became suddenly visible, periodically. Alyssia was convinced she could see groups of multicoloured butterfly-like insects hovering over the pools, and she asked Astara if they were butterflies of some kind.

"Indeed, you are seeing correctly," for the others in the Oswestry group couldn't imagine how she could have seen them from so far away, "you are seeing in a special way that the higher dimensions allow, since time and space are only relevant to lower levels. If you focus on something, it can seem close to you, for there is also no separation either, that separation which is often best in lower levels, of course!" she explained.

"Yes, you don't need to be 'on guard' at this level," agreed Alyssia, "and it is most interesting about the focusing technique."

The group were now trying to focus on distant points of interest now.

"What are those green beings over there?" asked Kenny, "near the mountains?" for some of the group were looking in the wrong places.

"Those are the elemental beings who oversee the lands around the Garden, and they bridge the gap between the fifth and sixth dimensions," said Aurial.

"How do they do that?" asked Karin.

"They constantly sing in a certain way that raises the vibratory level of the land around the Garden, in order to allow the Garden to remain in the sixth dimension, constantly," explained Aurial.

The mountains now ceased to have those pastel shades of pale blue and mauve, akin to objects on horizons, and the variety of foliage became increasingly more apparent. The luxuriant range of flowers were resplendent enough to attract many superlative comments.

"I've never seen so many flowers per square inch!" cried Sarah, "words fail me, it's so beautiful."

The Oswestry group were beginning to look overcome by such dazzling beauty that Zanadar flew forwards to talk to Aurial.

"Hadn't we better acclimatise our friends a little?" he asked, giving a glance towards the group.

"Yes, you're right," responded Aurial, "let us touch down in that clearing near the tarn."

"It does depend how residents from various planets react to the sixth dimension, for their metabolisms respond differently," commented Astara.

Aurastara gently guided the Oswestry group down to the tarn. The others gathered around alongside them. They were surrounded by more of the beautiful foliage. It was iridescent green, which sparkled as if from within the leaves. The flowers were the same, but they radiated in a rainbow light, multicoloured, with gold spangled light emanating from within the centres of the flowers. The Oswestry group looked very moved.

"Everything is so beautiful! I don't know why it's making me cry!" cried Alyssia, half laughing through her tears.

"It's the colours, and the fact that they are filled with light. They are so alive!" cried Sarah, looking amazed and moved at the same time.

"That's it!" said Karin.

"It's pure love, glowing from them," commented Kenny, turning away to try and hide his feelings.

"Yes indeed, all!" replied Aurastara, "it is the purity of these plants that is moving for you, and so you need to acclimatise yourselves."

"A good idea that will help you, is to have a bathe in this tarn, as you may call it," explained Astara, "these are the healing waters that border the Garden of Astragandara. If you'd like to change your clothes, Aurial will take you to the little hut, where you can leave your garments."

"Will it be cold?" asked Kenny, uncertainly.

"No, you will find it warm and invigorating!" replied Astara.

Aurial led them to the small hut made of interlaced branches, and drapes that were hung on the inside. Soon the group returned, and began to enter the water. Sarah resolutely walked briskly into it. Kenny sauntered to the edge and peered in cautiously. Karin and Alyssia walked upto the water's edge and tested it with their feet.

"Not bad! Let's go in!" said Alyssia.

"Ok, we'll go in together," answered Karin, "Kenny!"

Kenny smiled over, and walked into the water to join them.

"Look! The water has changed colour; it's pink and mauve!" cried Sarah, incredulously.

"It looks golden over here!" cried Alyssia.

"It's definitely turquoise!" answered Kenny.

Eventually, everyone quietened down and were floating around peacefully on their backs. The calming energy from the forest, already instilled into the water, was now infusing and percolating its way into their beings.

The group intuitively knew when they had had enough healing from the waters, and began to come out.
"I feel so peaceful now, a really strong peace," stated Sarah.
"I agree," responded Alyssia, "the water's energy is very strong, and I could feel a lot of love flowing through and around me!"
"I kept on getting the impression that our hearts were opening further to universal consciousness, to cope with the sixth dimension, and be able to accommodate it now," explained Karin.
"I just felt wonderful, an inexpressible state of being to describe adequately," said Kenny, with an animated expression.
"Well! It sounds as if all went very well for you all!" stated Aurial, and the other two, Astara and Aurastara smiled warmly. Aurastara indicated for the group to get changed.

Astara and Aurial concentrated deeply, while the group were getting changed. Gradually, it became apparent that something was on the horizon, floating over the treetops, and was approaching them swiftly.
Aurastara nodded as she watched the approaching spectacle, "Gloriae has them with her!" she exclaimed.
"Excellent!" cried the other two angelic beings.
The group returned from the changing hut to see the being approaching.
"This is Gloriae!" announced Aurial.
"Has she got the Glorae-astraespheres?" asked Alyssia, brightly.
"Indeed she has!" responded Aurial, "I wondered if you or Sarah would realise!"
Gloriae came to land next to them all. She was a slightly taller angelic being than the other three, since she dwelt by the Garden of Astragandara, and tended the bordering woodlands and waterways.
Apart from the brilliant light that emanated from her, as with all others, there were golden, dappled, star-like energies encircling her, as of the planet's energies, and also silver streaks dancing around her pale golden clothes, like sun-drenched watery ripples. Gloriae laughed melodiously, and approached the group. She held out her left hand, and smiled broadly. Two Glorae-astraespheres leapt from her hand, and went over to Sarah and Alyssia. They landed on their hands, glowing brightly.

"They look really happy!" exclaimed Alyssia, with an astonished smile.

"They are! They've been well energised in the Garden, along with many others," Gloriae replied.

Then Gloriae opened her right hand to reveal two more Gloraeastraespheres, which flew over to Karin and Kenny.

"We didn't want to leave you two out, and since you are on Astragandaran soil, we thought you deserved to have your own Glorae-astraespheres!"

"How wonderful, thank you!" cried Karin, with a radiant smile.

"They're so beautiful," said Kenny, engrossed in looking at his crystal.

"I think we are ready to proceed now, don't you?" said Aurial to the other angelic beings.

The group found bags to put their Glorae-astraespheres away, and then they all rose upwards, and continued onwards over the borderland woods before the Garden's domain would become visible to them.

The mountains were very close now, therefore, the Garden of Astragandara would be found very soon, and was obviously hidden amongst the mass of greenery that lay ahead of them, and which stretched upto the foot of the mountains.

At least, that's what the Oswestry group thought. It was with some surprise that they all flew straight over the woods, and then towards an aperture between two walls of rock that had craggy overhangs, resplendent with hanging gardens of golden tinged ferny plants.

"That gave you a surprise!" said Aurial; "we thought we'd keep it a secret, until now!"

The group looked intrigued.

"You see, if you were projecting your thoughts in anticipation of viewing this place, it may have caused some distraction to the Garden's energies, although such a domain isn't unduly affected, but your thought energies would be registered," explained Aurial, "and we are expected to keep such things minimal."

"You will soon know why our words are true!" said Aurastara with a smile.

They all began to move through the rocky aperture, and the light became more intense, with a rainbow-like quality to it. Everyone began to shimmer with this rainbow-light, and their eyes held this light in them, with a mellow-glow, which began to gradually increase as they progressed into the Garden.

Alyssia pointed suddenly. "Look at that!" she said.

A showering arc of golden light appeared in front of them.
"It is the Astragandaran energy in full force that is being shown here!" stated Aurial.
The Oswestry group smiled happily, with a depth of heartfelt joy and peace that was very strong, making their eyes glow even brighter.
Kenny wondered if any waterfalls would show up, and then his thoughts appeared in front of the group like a hologram, an image of water falling, complete with the sound effects, including the rustling of leaves and birdsong. The energy around them shimmered a bit, and became slightly less lustrous and bright, and then the thought image faded, and the atmosphere turned brighter again.
"Oh dear," cried Kenny, "that didn't help the energies of this place."
"Don't worry! It was a good demonstration of what we meant with regard to keeping it secret," responded Aurial, "just keep thoughts to a minimum."
They all flew further along, and came to a bend, and everyone gasped at the beauty before them. There were masses of magnificent flowers and trees, with natural walkways here and there. Also, Zanadar, Aurion and Salaron were there, waiting for them, for they had continued onwards when the Oswestry group had gone bathing in the tarn. They had been so preoccupied; they hadn't noticed their departure.
"It is the essence of stillness that keeps the purity here, stillness of mind and so on," explained Aurastara.
They all landed beside the space beings. They expected to talk to one another telepathically, but were all consumed by the still atmosphere so much that communication became irrelevant, and they all smiled to each other knowingly.

As they looked at each other, a silver-golden sheen appeared around them all, as a whole, and it was like they knew each other at a deeper level than previously. As if they had all become a unit of consciousness.
"This is the sixth dimension, there is no separation!" explained Aurial, gently, "we are treading in Divine realms now."
The angelic beings indicated for everyone to follow them along a particular pathway, but everyone had known what the angelic beings had intended, before they said, since they were all linked together.

As they walked along, they brushed past the huge flowering trees, of which the blossoms were an impressive size, almost three feet wide on the lower branches, but the petals were thin, almost translucent, so they didn't weigh as much as those would on a three dimensional planet. Their centres glowed with an inner light, and it was all the Oswestry group could do, to stop themselves from being swallowed up by their fascinating appearance. Not to mention the elusively beautiful scent, and hints of melody that they wafted past them, periodically. The angelic beings had to keep calling the groups' names every so often to keep the whole group moving, as each of them kept stopping at the flowers.

"We are on the outskirts of the Garden of Astragandara, and will come to a variety of places on the way through to the final point," explained Aurial.

Through the luxuriant, tree-lined pathways, a break, which was quite uncharacteristic, allowed a view through to a distant peak. It had a verdant slope up towards the summit, with gold tinged flowers.

"What are those things flying around the mountains?" asked Alyssia.

"There are many butterflies and birds that love to be up the sides of our mountains, and Mount Gandera is no exception!" replied Astara.

Kenny and Karin were deep in thought together, and then Sarah noticed, put her hand on Karin's shoulder, and spoke to them.

"You two are looking very preoccupied!" she said.

"Yes," replied Karin, slowly, "you see, we are wondering how all this will tie into our overall mission or intent. How we can bring all this wisdom from the past and the future to our own time."

"Yes, I'd almost forgotten about this, while experiencing all that we have done," replied Sarah, "somehow I'd thought the answers would just come naturally, during our adventures."

Alyssia was flying overhead and joined in too.

"It is true, we haven't found out how to process it all, to present to the world, as yet," said Alyssia.

They all turned to look at Zanadar, Aurion, and Salaron.

"We know, don't let it worry you as yet," replied Zanadar, his orange-pink face was reassuringly cheerful, as usual.

"This planet holds many keys, indeed!" said Salaron.

"And you haven't been into the future yet, either!" added Aurion, and he gave an enigmatic smile, which made the Oswestry group feel strangely intrigued.

"Is it that we may see the future from Astragandara?" queried Sarah.

"You could be onto something there, Sarah!" quipped Kenny.

The space beings and the angelic beings began to laugh cheerfully, which eventually made the Oswestry group laugh too. The laughter left an ever-increasing lightness in the group's hearts, as they progressed onwards. There was a branching route to the path, and they all turned to go up towards the mountain.
"Can we fly there?" asked Karin.
"What's wrong with a bit of exercise, dear?" said Kenny, with a smile.
"Well, I thought it might be nice to look around the mountain," replied Karin, "from above."
"Remember the rocky crevice we entered through?" said Aurial, pointing in its direction, "you will see it when we are up on top, and the mountains as an encircling ring of peaks. We do have quite a lot to cover, so a bit of help would be an advantage."
"You can walk if you like, Kenny!" said Aurastara, jovially.
"Ok then, I'll join the majority!" laughed Kenny.
"Let's go!" cried Aurial, and she rose by ten feet in an instant.
Everyone else did the same, and then they focused on the grassy slopes of the mountain, and in the next instance, they found themselves right there, standing amongst the green, gold-tinged grasses, watching the multicoloured butterflies fluttering around.
"There's some of those lovely flowers, what were they called?" asked Karin.
"Spanglefoil!" answered Astara.
"Those butterflies have wings like transparent lace," said Alyssia, examining some on the spanglefoil flowers. Then they lifted off and flew around Alyssia, with a faintly melodic hum, and then they were joined by another dozen of them, which flew around the whole group, and finally disappeared off down the mountainside.
"The flowers look more resplendent since the butterflies have passed by, I'm sure of it!" said Sarah, who looked amazed.
"You are right," affirmed Aurial, "the butterflies have drunk the nectar, but have appeared to pollinate the plants like they do on Earth. It always enlivens plants on three-dimensional planets, but there is no need to do this here, though they do enjoy an exchange of energy, like a sharing of love that energises the plants. Somehow, like many actions on planets that are at higher levels, these energies are filtered down to lower frequencies."
"How lovely!" replied Sarah, and the rest of the group soundly agreed.

They continued to the summit, and could see the vista of the Garden, the bordering regions encircling it, and the rest of the planet beyond that. Those golden showers seen when coming to land on the planet were plain to see, once at a higher altitude. Like an aurora borealis of golden showers, or a firework display of a soft and gentle nature, everyone could see that it was continuous.
"I wondered what that sound was, like a hum that comes with every shower," cried Alyssia.
Alyssia turned to look at the others, with a sudden realisation.
"It's a manifestation of the universal sound," whispered the Oswestry group in unison, looking awed and moved again.
"Absolutely spectacular, it never ceases to impress us, either," smiled Zanadar.
They stood for a while, watching the showers surging across the pale, golden-white sky, and every time a shower came across, a pearlescent glow appeared in the sky in its wake. Then a flock of multicoloured birds flew by, echoing a series of liquid melodic notes several times over. They circled the mountain three times, and wheeled off down into the Garden area, to land amongst some of the trees.
"It is time to move off, my friends!" said Aurial; "we still have a number of places to visit."
"Where shall we visit next?" asked Kenny.
"Something familiar to some!" smiled Aurial, enigmatically, not far away!"

They all hovered gently down the side of the mountain, to where a small river could be seen amongst the trees, at the base, and they walked down the pathway into the forest again. The pathway led along to a little bridge over the river, with a carefully carved number of rails and uprights, and then the path rose up out of the forest again, around the side of the adjacent peak to Mount Gandera.

Together the visiting group held a feeling of anticipation, and then the intuitive knowing of what they were going to visit.
"We are going to visit a group of large crystals, aren't we?" asked Sarah, with an animated gleam in her eyes.
"Correct!" everyone else replied, and then they all laughed, since they all knew the answer at the same time!
"It's getting harder to keep anything as a surprise in this dimension, as you all become accustomed to it!" said Aurial, jovially.

They rounded a corner in the forest pathway that was filled with glorious pearly-tinged emerald-green leaves, and pearl-tinged petals, all humming melodiously. There was a little clearing ahead, and with the sunlight illuminating them, stood a circle of crystals, and they were glowing so brightly, it was hard for the Oswestry group to look at them.
"If I'd known, I would have brought our sunglasses!" cried Kenny, squinting like the others.
"It will be fine, just walk towards them, and you will see," explained Aurastara.
So they proceeded, and as they all entered the circle, the intensity of the glow around the crystals began to soften.
"The crystals are humming a variety of sounds, as well as that Aum note," said Alyssia, "are they communicating?"
"Yes, they do communicate," answered Aurastara, and she gave a meaningful look, "do you remember the crystal mountain?"
"Of course! I don't know how I could have forgotten!" cried Alyssia, "all that way! Sarah!"
"I know, it's incredible!" cried Sarah.
"And wonderful!" added Karin.
"I had wished I'd been there, but I'm having a chance to experience it now!" commented Kenny, happily, "are there other places these crystals link with?"
"Yes there are, with neighbouring planets, including Reluisia, in this sphere, and then the energy can radiate out to more distant planets. For the energy usually is sent via a chain of planets, to reach the furthest ones. Occasionally, if all is favourable, we can link in directly, as in Lemurian times," explained Astara.
"How do you manage to link directly to the planet?" asked Kenny.
"It's all down to which Age is in progress," replied Astara, "the Golden Age allows a better conducting of energies over long distances, a better frequency level."

They went and sat in the middle of the crystal circle, and began to feel the energy there in motion, and sat a while. Later, Alyssia, Sarah and Karin began a discussion and Kenny joined in.
"We can all see energy going off towards other planets," said Kenny, after the discussion, "we were discussing about which planets the energy was going to, and whether we could sense that."
"Did you manage to decipher which was which?" asked Aurastara.

"We decided that we could tell, because there was an energy link to the receiving planet, and intuited its presence that way!" explained Karin.
"That's one of the best ways to do it," said Aurial.

With that, the crystals began to glow again, and as well as being a hub for energy activation for many planets, the crystal circle was giving energy to the group as well. Flame-like fire played around all their energy systems, charging it up, and activating layers of the aura that would enhance greater insightfulness. The group were deeply linked to the crystals, and felt as one with them, and could interpret the energy's effects on the recipient planets. How their energy alignment would pull them towards the fifth dimension at some point in their destinies, because of that link to spirit and the guidance that resulted from it, because, apart from the energy flow, thought streams of the universe would come through those energy lines, like inner messages, positive thought forms that would be in such constant flow, that its effect would eventually permeate through, bringing a stream of wisdom with it. This link would naturally be with planets of the same dimension, to emphasise the efficiency of energy transmission, and to maintain those planets to that level as well.

Alyssia, like the others in their group, opened her eyes after contemplation, and they were filled with a brighter energy still, and a blazing mass of dancing lights shining from her eyes. The others opened their eyes, and looked at one another, startled by this transfiguration in their eyes as well.
"I can see each planet, where the light streams from the Source go," said Alyssia.
"I hear Aum sounds, and within that are pulses of other melodies," remarked Sarah.
"I can hear impressions, easily translated into words, such as – the beings who run our universe are the guiding force, and they initiate the light streams into moving as they do between many planets," explained Karin.
"I got the impression that, of course, the energy primarily goes into the planets themselves, first, before reaching out to individuals from insects to humanoids on the various planets," said Kenny.
"Well spoken," said Aurial, "you are all coming along very well."
"Yes, indeed," agreed Aurastara, her eyes also held that radiant, sparkling light. "Now we will make our way to the next destination, which is a waterfall."

They all left the crystal circle. Zanadar pointed over beyond the area they were standing at, to where there was a break in the trees, and a glimpse through to a long valley was visible, that lay in the opposite direction to Mount Gandera, from where they had begun the trail. Everyone gathered around to have a good look.

"That is where the waterfall will be found," explained Aurastara, "it will be a bit further on than the distance from the mountain, but it's a beautiful walk, you'll love it!"

There were responses from the group such as, "lovely!" "Can't wait!" and "I'll paint that!"

"Where do you think you lived when you were here?" asked Aurion of Alyssia and Sarah.

"I've not thought about it yet, though the area we set out from seemed familiar," said Sarah.

Aurion looked at Alyssia, expectantly.

"I'm not sure either, and I'm hoping this journey out here will help me to see," replied Alyssia, "I must say, having said that, I feel great kinship with the crystals and the Garden area, however."

"I'm sure you'll both remember soon enough," replied Aurion, reassuringly.

"This flower may be part of that remedy!" exclaimed Zanadar, who was standing beside an exquisitely delicate, rainbow-lit flower head, and beckoned to Alyssia and Sarah, and they came over with Aurion. "Smell this," he said.

Alyssia and Sarah took turns in inhaling the perfume, and they both looked deeply meditative, but also a bit dazed by the intensity of its effect.

"I could see into the past, I think," explained Alyssia, "I was looking around the forests and I noticed that my feet were bare, and my skin was a golden colour. I had crystals in my hands, and a bag was around my waist, and I looked at it, and just peeping out of the top of the bag was one of those flower heads!"

Zanadar and Aurion looked interested, and then looked at Sarah.

"I could hear the roar of a waterfall, and expected to find myself back in Atlantis, but no, this was a different one, with glorious golden plants around it, but all different species, and I was drying some of the leaves in the sun. I had a bag with me, and I was aware that it held some of the herbs," explained Sarah.

Both Alyssia and Sarah looked moved on discovering these glimpses, of their lives on Astragandara.

"We must have been healers!" cried Alyssia.

"Yes, my love of waterfalls runs very deep!" said Sarah.
They both smiled gently, with a slightly wistful expression, and their eyes still held that rainbow sparkle.
"You've truly come home!" said Karin, giving Sarah and Alyssia a quick hug, and Kenny hugged them too.
"Now you know, do you know where you can get some biscuits around here?" asked Kenny, with an expression of jocular earnestness.
Everyone laughed, including the angelic beings.
"We'll have to create a recipe for a golden biscuit just for you!" said Aurial.
"Oh good!" replied Kenny with a broad grin.

The walk through the woods was accompanied by many of those rainbow-lit flowers. Galaxy plants was the name of them, because of the far-reaching capacity they held for universal knowledge and understanding. At a brow of a hill, they could all see and hear the waterfall, and the view opened out a bit more, as the forest thinned out, with areas of it further away either side of the group, as they continued to walk over to the falls area. As the view opened out, they could see that the water came down the side of one of the encircling mountains in three separate torrents, due to the geography of the rocky overhang above. It then fell into a series of pools, each slightly lower than the next, as the water ran downwards into a lower valley, and that river torrent was lined with many golden tinged trees. Curiously, there was an island in the midst of the waterfalls' pools, just where they ran into the beginning of the river. The group began to notice the mass of golden plants surrounding the edges of the pools, and some were on the island as well.
"What a beautiful place!" cried Alyssia.
"Absolute heaven!" stated Sarah.
"Can we get over to the island?" asked Karin.
"Yes, but you have to know what the plant is that's on it, first!" replied Astara.
"Why is that, please?" asked Karin.
"Because of the effects it has. It is a very powerful herb," responded Astara.
"We'll explain shortly," said Aurial, and she walked to the herbs by the pool side, "come, I wish to tell you about these herbs, and what they're good for."
Everyone duly went and sat on the gold tinged, green grass, gently warmed by the sun, and faced Aurial.
The spangly light of the sun appeared reflected in Aurial's eyes, as well as everyone else's. So, that bright light in their eyes

seemed magnified. All people and beings who came to Astragandara found their eyes taking on the same look. Due, of course, to the radiant golden energy that permeated everything on the planet.

"I have to tell you that these herbs are widely distributed to neighbouring planets, and the juice of these is that well-known effervescent liquid that you have drunk many times!" explained Aurial, with a smile.

The group were duly exclaiming surprise.

"Does it grow widely throughout Astragandara?" asked Sarah.

"Indeed! It grows by our many waterfalls, for it likes to be by water that is churned up and frothy," commented Aurial.

Sarah examined the leaves of the plant in question, which had bold, but lacy edged leaves, and the flowers were tall and upright, with petals that were held close together, and a lip at the top of each petal.

"Does this liquid come from the leaves or roots? Asked Sarah.

"Ah! I didn't give you all the information, as we wanted Sarah to remember about this, and ask more questions," replied Aurial, "the liquid comes from inside the flower, which oozes from the interior of the flower during the night, and we collect it in the early morning."

There was another plant nearby, which was low growing, creeping along like an ivy, except that it was golden in colour, as usual, and Aurial turned her attention to it now.

"This plant is used for those of us who travel between dimensions a great deal," explained Aurial.

"I do believe they were the leaves presented to me in the dining hall!" exclaimed Kenny.

"Very true, and they would have been useful!" smiled Aurial, "try some leaves now, everyone!"

They all helped themselves gently to several leaves, and chewed them. Immediately new leaves grew back, from where they were taken.

"I can't quite say how it has affected me," said Sarah, "but I feel a bit more alert, I think!"

"Maybe the plant fine tunes you to wherever you are," commented Kenny.

"Yes exactly, that is what it does," stated Aurial.

"You especially need it when returning to lower frequencies, my friends," said Aurastara.

"We will give you a supply to return with," said Astara, "we have our supplies ready dried near the dining hall."

"Now you can try that island!" announced Aurial.

There were able to float easily over to the island amid the resident island plant, which was quite large. The Oswestry group talked amongst themselves swiftly.

"We think it is like the elixir plant we were given via the caskets," stated Sarah.

"It is very much like the elixir or nourishing plant, because it helps us give its substance to our visitors, like Zanadar and all, who can use it on their travels when moving between dimensions," explained Aurial, "it holds a lot of energy, and of the highest dimensions, so it not only affects you physically, but spiritually also."

Aurastara and Astara flew back onto the bank again, and beckoned everyone to follow, which they did.

"Now we are going down past the river, and then we shall see a lake there, and that is our next stop," said Aurastara.

With that, the three angelic beings rose up and floated along beside the river. The others followed, and then they all rose to above the tree height and sped along, with the river below them. The river was gradually getting lower, and it went over a series of cascades, and then levelled out a bit more, and finally began to meander slightly.

The group were looking down at the river quite a lot, and didn't notice they were approaching the lake, until Aurial brought it to their attention. Soon they came to land beside it, and they marvelled at its rainbow-tinted waters, with golden sparkling lights dancing in it. A dreamy feeling emanated from the water, and a murmuring kind of melody was just audible to the Oswestry group.

"You do know that in this dimension, water is not the same as in your third one. Put your hand into the water and see!" said Astara.

Everyone in the Oswestry group did so, not noticing initially that Zanadar and the other space beings did not need to, since they knew the outcome already.

"It doesn't feel the same, it's not wet!" cried Alyssia.

"It's more like a mist, somehow," remarked Karin.

"Yes, and you can, in fact, walk through it, and still breathe well enough," explained Astara.

"Does that mean we're going in?" asked Sarah.

"Yes!" replied Aurial, "it's very lovely in the lake!"

"Come on, just follow me!" ushered Aurastara.

She stepped in and encouraged the others to follow. Zanadar, Aurion and Salaron flanked them all reassuringly. As the water level rose, they could feel it around them like a misty, warm and smooth emanation, with its opalescent look, and golden sparkles gently swirling around them. The water level reached their heads, but the Oswestry group still instinctively looked a bit apprehensive.

"Don't worry! Just breathe as normal, as you don't need to do anything else," emphasised Aurial.

As the water covered their heads, they realised all was fine, and they could see each other and the terrain they were walking over, down a pathway between rocky outcrops. They were surrounded by those opalescent swirls, and little fish-like beings floated around, tending to small plants on the lake bottom.

"Those are a kind of undine, and they work for the regular kind of undine you know of, you'll probably see some soon," commented Astara.

As they progressed, they became aware of certain currents of energy entering the lake, from the river that flowed from the waterfall, and from other rivers too. Some parts of the lake bed were quite deep, with chasms here and there, but the group continued along on their particular pathway. They rounded a bend, over another outcrop area, and to the Oswestry group's surprise, there stood a group of small buildings made of stones. Aurial went to the first one and called inside, and a tall and willowy being with flowing attire came to the door.

"Hello Aurial, and everyone, please come inside, we've been expecting you," the being said.

As they went in, they were greeted by a group of others like the being at the door, the Oswestry group 'knew' they were the devas of the area, who oversaw the undines and other elementals. The first willowy being drew everyone inside, and they all became seated.

"Now," said the first willowy being, looking at the Oswestry group, "my name is linked with all the others of my kind here, and are called the Sentinel, like the Garden of Eden in Atlantis, and we all think as one unit. There are things you should know, to take back to your own time period, and some beings wish to offer their wisdom. I'll invite them in!"

She turned her head, as did the rest of the Sentinel, and intoned their intention in unison. A small side door opened, that was about half the height of the front entrance, and a variety of beings came in, elves, fairies and gnomes, who all looked remarkably similar to the ones on Earth, except for the golden glow in their eyes and about their person. They came and sat in front of the Sentinel, opposite the Oswestry group.

"Hello!" said Kenny, happily, and then the rest of the group joined in.

"Welcome to our world!" cried the elementals in response.

The group smiled and looked expectantly. Alyssia fleetingly glanced towards the space beings behind them, and they were in deep meditation, then they all realised everyone else was also in deep meditation, so they composed themselves and followed suit.

Alyssia saw the depths below them, and the Gaia-like being of the planet. "You must know the depths of peace in your heart, before you can realise anything else, as it casts the right resonance, and like an ascending lift, if you are at the ground floor, you won't see anything on the first or second floors until you are able to lift to those levels!"

"What are on those levels that we are to see?" asked Alyssia, as she could feel her heart growing ever more peaceful.

"You will know soon enough!" came the reply.

Sarah saw herself with her herbs, giving offerings to temples around Astragandara, and sent many a herb over to other worlds for healing and insights.

"You and your friends have helped, with your work done in past lives, and endeavours in this life with the caskets. Know that you are being rewarded by coming here, and you must know this information to take back with you," said the Gaia being.

Karin linked in, and could see images of stars above her, as she was bringing through thoughts from somewhere even higher than Astragandara. 'Be still, I am the Source of your Universe. Know that I am closer to you than any part of your physical body. I am the fulcrum of existence, get to know me well!'

Kenny could see the energy of the planet's Source, emanating from various places like golden fountains, helped by the nature spirits, and streams of it were running from place to place. 'Astragandaran ley lines!' thought Kenny. 'Linking the fifth dimension with the sixth,' came a thought, and then Kenny could see many nature spirits round him, smiling.

The group began to return to the room they were in, all had heard the words that Alyssia had given to her, and the words 'you must know the depths of peace in your heart,' recurred several times, as they were withdrawing from their meditation. Aurial, Aurastara and Astara, who were seated with the Sentinel, looked over and smiled animatedly. The nature spirits looked over too, their golden sheen eyes seemed mesmerising to the group, and they felt drawn in. The space beings sat, with eyes slightly closed in a respectful silence, knowing that this interchange was most beneficial. The Sentinel were concentrating on keeping the energy of the room extremely still. Alyssia, Karin, Sarah and Kenny were aware of a vast green light around them, filled with golden streams, radiating in all directions. The faces of all kinds of elementals came and went, including the Sentinel and the Gaia-like being again. The energy radiated through them all, and increased in intensity, and then gently subsided again, and they all came out of meditation and opened their eyes.

Everyone asked the Oswestry group how they were feeling, and awaited responses. The group looked at each other, and they all knew how deeply they felt.
Sarah spoke, "I speak for all of us, and we feel such deep peace, and know how much Astragandara's energies affect the rest of the universe, and how deeply it links to Verdamara and Reluisia, but we can also see a map of the universe, and how all is linked together, and can be brought up anytime. Also, as well as that, we feel a deeply glowing force of vast intelligence pervading our every conscious moment, showering infinite love into our midst, as well as everyone else's, if they would know it!"
"Well spoken, and we are so glad that you are perceiving well!" replied the Sentinel and nature spirits.
"It is time to move on to the next place now, everyone!" said Aurial, Aurastara and Astara.
Everyone got up and exchanged greetings and hugs, and those who visited, made their way through the swirling rainbow energy of the lake once more. They found they were accompanied by some undines.
"We were gathered around the exterior of the building you meditated inside, and were glad you could come!"
Their eyes held that golden sheen, and their clothes were diaphanous, with plant-like fronds billowing out around them. The group weren't sure if they were plants or part of the clothing. The undines smiled sweetly and said they were actually plants.

Once out of the lake, they were greeted by a view that held a brighter, and more shimmering sparkle to it than beforehand.
"Where are we visiting next?" asked Sarah.
"Our well is next, and then there are two other places, some standing stones and a cave," replied Astara.
"The well isn't far away, and is just a bit further on past the lake," said Aurial.
"Can we fly there?" asked Alyssia, turning to see everyone else's responses, which were affirming her question.

"Let's go!" cried Aurial, and they all took off, and were soon at the far end of the lake. They waved to a group of elves who were bringing good energy into the roots of some large viridian trunked trees at the head of the lake. They proceeded along a winding pathway, and as they could see that it narrowed increasingly, they had landed, and were walking the remainder of the way to the well.

There in a little clearing stood the well. It was completely surrounded by a thick bed of gold tinged, viridian shaded moss. The water was like the lake, filled with a rainbow sheened aura, with the usual golden sparkles everywhere. Here and there, myriads of tiny lace-winged beings flitted about, with tiny, brilliant white balls of energy. These white balls of energy emanated from the well, as periodically, the golden sparkles increased in intensity, and shimmering white light oozed out of the water, accompanied with a chant like resonance, and the tiny beings formed it into balls, and flew off in all directions, taking this energy far and wide.
"These are like your fairies, and they take this essence to trees, plants, stones, anything that needs more sustenance to grow, or increase its energy levels," explained Aurastara.
The fairies then brought a ball each to the Oswestry group, who looked quite moved by the experience. The fairies held their balls of energy out, and the group took them in their hands, and knew that they just had to hold it to their hearts, and the energy would be assimilated.
"Come and lie down by the well everyone!" cried Astara.
"I enjoy lying down here, it's so restful," said Zanadar.
None of us would miss any opportunity to do so!" added Aurion.
There was enough room for everyone to lie radially around the well, so that their feet were near the well, and heads and bodies arranged like spokes in a wheel. They all shut their eyes, and immediately a gentle but sonorous melody became apparent. It lulled them into a meditative state, and there was deep peace and such stillness that the group felt that thought was unnecessary. Peace radiated through them all. As the group opened their eyes, they could see all the spirits of every tree, flower, stone, water, and also ones on the mountains, when glimpses of them could be seen, as well as those in the air, and many other spirits who inhabited Astragandara's Garden.
"Now you can see even more," stated Aurial, "these beings are from nearer the Source, and are part of the sixth dimension and beyond, and they bring their energy to bear here."

They all got up slowly, and knew to continue along the pathway, for they had all seen a glimpse of where the standing stones could be found. The forest was full of the flowering trees, as usual, yet these ones had jewel-like drops of nectar, which caught the sunlight like crystal gems, sparkling with a rainbow sheen. A myriad of multicoloured butterflies of the Astragandaran variety were fluttering around those rainbow sheened drops of nectar. Now, an Astragandaran butterfly has a wing span four to six times larger than those on Earth, and the patterns on their wings are more intricate still, and as well as the colourings of the markings, and there is that golden and opalescent sheen on them.

Everyone was happy to walk along, quietly looking around at everything, which was absorbing their attention. The path curved here and there, went over a few areas of raised ground, and several streams. Then the ground began to rise more increasingly, until they reached the brow of a hill, and there before them, stood a small group of standing stones. The stones were covered in moss and lichen, and they were surrounded by huge plants, a bit like giant moss, with lots of feathery ended leaves, and water absorbing branches and trunks, which made them very sturdy and bulbous looking, also with a damp patina to them.
"Just touch the stones, strangely there is one each for you, the Oswestry group!" said Aurial.
As the Oswestry group each stood beside a stone, looking across at each other, and then focused on the stone in front of each of them. The stones began to glow, and a radiant energy was apparent for being held there. Energy radiated from the stones out to the surrounding countryside on one side. On the other, it went uphill slightly, disappearing through the trees, and the group initially wondered where to, then they knew, it was to the cave.
Beings of light converged on the area, but they sped overhead in the direction of the cave. The Oswestry group stopped what they were doing, and the whole group knew they must go to that cave now, but no one needed to speak, as if a meditative state was all-important to maintain for this final destination.

Chapter 11 - Where all the Universe Meets

The group continued onwards in silence, picking their way through the opalescent sheen on the blossomed trees, complete with radiant butterflies. Alyssia and Karin looked amazed when a group of the butterflies began to hum a beautiful melody. Then they knew, it was because they were approaching the cave. It was impressed upon all the Oswestry group to approach the cave especially quietly and gently, for the energy there was even more finely tuned. Through more trees they went, and then the foliage thinned out, and they came to a wall of yellow, sandy rock, with the characteristic gold sheen to it. Aurial beckoned for them all to turn right and make their way along, which they did for a few minutes, and then the rocky wall receded, and they were all confronted by an intriguing entrance in the rock face. It had an open doorway, carved directly into the rock, and an aperture was visible inside it.

Once everyone had grouped together, Aurial, Astara and Aurastara beckoned for them all to approach the cave entrance. They had expected it to be dark inside, with maybe a light or fire lit here and there, but they were surprised to see the whole area illuminated, as if with a light from the higher dimensions. Zanadar went in first, followed by Sarah and Alyssia, Karin and Kenny, the other space beings and the three angelic beings. They stood in an ante-chamber, and Aurial came to the front and guided the group onwards. They proceeded along a passageway that went downwards, down many stone-carved steps to a doorway. Aurial placed her hand on the door, which opened, and she entered, indicating for the others to follow.

They all entered a large oval room, which was a temple area. An altar had been carved out of the rock face, and a small underground stream ran along a runnel at the back of the room, passing underneath the altar, and splaying out into a pool area beside it. The oval shape of the room was at its widest to the left and right sides of the entrance, and the ground sloped upwards at the sides, so again, seats and benches had been carved out of the rock there. Everyone noticed a strongly fragrant smell, of some kinds of herbs or flowers. A priestly figure stood at the far end, and he had the golden sheen in his eyes, and a pale golden skin, only to be expected on Astragandara, and he also wore a golden robe. The group wondered fleetingly about the beings of light who had come in the direction of the cave, but they then immediately knew the beings weren't far away. The priest smiled benignly and indicated for everyone to sit down. He then began to radiate blessings out on the group, the temple space, Astragandara, and upon the session that was about to begin. He went to a casket beside the altar, and picked out some incense, which he ignited, and a fresh wave of that strongly fragrant smell began to pervade the temple. He then turned to face everyone again and he looked intently at the wall, to one of the corner areas, to the left of the altar.

A light appeared, and everyone immediately thought of what usually happens in Anchorin's temple. They saw a small temple, set in grounds, its top a lilac shade, blending into pink at its base, and then they were inside it, and they could see Anui, Deanu and Giana looking towards them. The three of them smiled, and a symbol was projected from them, and it came into the temple, hanging suspended in front of everyone. It emanated a sparkling, golden light, and everyone knew that it had the depth of the essence's capacity, and link to the Divine Source within it. The Oswestry group could feel its energy moving through them, and knew that it held the emerald spark of creation, for all dimensions in its midst. That was about as much as they could apprehend at that moment.

The image faded, and then more light appeared in its place. Amid a bright emerald coloured mass of greenery, a bright landscape of light emerged. A large temple was apparent, surrounded by other smaller ones, then they could see inside the temple, and the three female guardian beings, with their brightly illumined eyes shone into the temple space where the Oswestry group were sitting. The light seemed to permeate everyone's minds in that temple area, filtering into their hearts and all of their beings. It was as if they found the universe was inside them, glowing as brightly as the three guardians' eyes in the temple over the Verdamaran Garden of Eden. Then the light faded, and everyone sat quietly in contemplation.
"Now it is time to adjourn to the temple of crystal light," said the priest, and beckoned for the group to follow him.

They followed the priest through an arched door at the back of the temple, behind the altar, and up a staircase of obsidian. Alyssia and Sarah looked at each other, remembering the crystal mountain. At the top of the staircase, everyone could see large stars blazing brightly. Once they were up a few steps, they realised that the sides of a structure surrounded them, and it had six facets, and was transparent. It was a huge crystal, and about twenty feet high, and this was identical to the astral travelling experience Alyssia and Sarah had at the crystal mountain. As they both realised this, echoed by amazed expressions, everyone's Glorae-astraespheres began to glow extremely brightly, and dazzled them. There was a resonant humming sound, that appeared to emanate from the giant crystal, and once everyone noticed, it became a glorious, unearthly chorus.

As they reached the top of the stairs, the priest, who had by now, impressed on everyone that his name was Gandar, ushered everyone to seats, carved from parts of the crystal, and they were arranged around a platform area, where they could all continue with the ceremony, or whatever else was to occur. They all sat together, with Gandar standing opposite. There were still some spare seats, and an air of expectation inevitably meant that other beings were going to come and sit on them.

Sure enough, the Oswestry group were amazed to see Siral, Maeron and Golan coming up the crystal steps, followed by other beings from the Council of Twelve, who the Oswestry group had not met before. Siral and Maeron were tall and streamlined, whereas Golan was short and squarish, with a jovial expression. The first of the other beings was rounded, like a Buddha, with the same gently contented look, and he was Gelsior from Pollux, next was Talar from Betelgeuse who was small and slight, with a bluish skin, and Gillan from Antares had a strong and purposeful expression, and was stocky and tall. From Lyra was Melkior, who was dark-skinned with pale green eyes, calm and noble, and was closely followed by Kelaré from Ursa Major, who was small, wiry, and animated, and he was linked to the Light Year Command. Finally, came Sikaron from Castor, who was a tall being surrounded in white light, gentle and meditative.

They all sat down next to the others, awaiting what would happen next. Gandar was looking to the heavens expectantly, from which a rush of light bore down towards the crystal's apex, and hovered overhead. Kelaré glanced at Gandar and without a word; everyone knew it was the Light Year Command, who mentors younger planets across many galaxies. There was a suffusion of light that enveloped everyone, and a meeting of minds was about to happen.
"We of the Light Year Command bridge the gap between time periods, past, present and future for all dimensions. For our

visitors from planet Earth, we especially invite you to a glimpse of your planet's future. By seeing this, you will know a deeper sense of purpose for people and other occupants. If you would just adopt a position of meditation, we will bring through the necessary information."

The Oswestry group had been pondering on why they were told that the sixth and seventh dimensions would not be encountered, but yet they had encountered a little of the sixth dimension. So much was happening that they didn't get around to asking the question! They immediately understood that it was due to their progress, that they were allowed to experience it to a degree. A beam of energy came down over the four members of the Oswestry group, with various smaller beams of patterned light within that, not dissimilar to a projector's light beam in a cinema.

The group could see images of the Earth in present times, becoming more affected by pollution, wars and degradation of all kinds. On the other hand, there was a growing band of those who genuinely cared for the Earth, and all manner of spiritual wisdom. They were continually moving to the areas of the planet best suited for their purposes, and little did they know, that their moves would help to stabilise the atmosphere, and ensure that spirituality would prosper. Especially when the time came for the release of the souls who cannot aspire to the higher dimensions, the spiritual ones would be safe where they were. The changes would come through the usual earthquakes and disastrous occurrences, as well as disease pandemics. The Earth would also move into an axial shift, gradually, so that America would be in the position of mid Atlantic, and Britain would be over where Greece is positioned.

Refocusing on the countries after such a time, they saw the caring people now rebuilding their lives, forming small communities of like-minded people, with healers, channellers, artists and writers, all joining together to form healing centres, with spiritual art, writing, poetry and performances. Other communities would have environmental organisations, herbalists, house and furniture builders and much else. The group noticed that some aspects of technology had survived, but was being adapted into new ways, where no damage to the Earth would occur. There was an increase in the energy around the group, as the images faded, and the group realised that the Light Year Command, and all the others in the crystal were resonating a huge amount of energy. This allowed the group to see how much everything was part of the overall plan, and younger planets always come to a stage of maturity at some point, and often at a critical moment, where in times past, many such opportunities to progress could not be taken by the inhabitants as a whole, only by individuals, but the latter were helping to show the former what could be done in due course, and was about to happen for Earth.

Everyone then moved down into the temple region again, and became seated, as Gandar invoked the light on the far wall again. As the group looked at it, an image of the Earth became visible, and then it homed in on Britain, which was tilted over slightly, like every other country.

Gandar came forward to the Oswestry group with a purposeful expression.
"Now! As you can see, we have Britain in a future time period," he announced, "the time is about 2,300AD in your time, and it is when the new order of life is beginning to assert itself. Would you like to visit this time period, and learn what it is really like? By this method you are able to look around and see what is going on, without becoming immersed in three dimensional life, so you are ethereally there."
"Yes we would like to go," replied Kenny, for all their minds linked together with that affirmative intent.
"Please step forward," said Gandar, and so they did. He looked to Zanadar and indicated for him to accompany them, so Zanadar stepped forward as well. "Now, just approach the wall one by one, that's right. Let Zanadar go first if you prefer."
Zanadar duly walked past everyone, stood in front of the wall where the illumined image was. Gandar ensured that the image was at ground level, within a clearing. The Oswestry group looked at him questioningly, and Gandar knew without words that they were enquiring how the wall images changed.
"I can change the imagery by using my mind," explained Gandar, "for I know these time periods quite well, and on other planets also!"
Zanadar turned and went through the wall, and could be seen on the other side, beckoning the others to come. Alyssia approached, and as her foot went to the wall, the whole of the structure became amorphous, and like pushing through a layer of cottage cheese, she said later, but without any dampness or anything adhering to oneself. The rest of the group went through, looking all around themselves.

"It's quite warm, not like our usual weather patterns," said Sarah.
"The air feels different, I can't say how, though," said Karin.
"It's the light, there's almost a violet tinge to it, and it's brighter," said Alyssia.
"Look over there, just between those trees," said Kenny, pointing, "I can see a building!"
They were all able to hover over the ground, which was grassy, with many shrubs and small trees everywhere. They moved between the larger trees until they came to the building, though there were a few buildings there, in fact, but they were dilapidated. A sign hung from one corner, and the group went over to scrutinise it.
"It says the Trading Corner!" said Kenny, with a puzzled expression, and he looked at Karin, and then the others. "That shop we always get al kinds of useful items from."
"But where is the rest of Oswestry?" queried Sarah, "it can't have all disappeared."
"Perhaps the stone has been carried off elsewhere," suggested Alyssia, "the way it has happened in various time periods."
"Ok, shall we explore around?" asked Karin.
Zanadar watched everyone's reactions calmly, with a gentle smile, and followed them all onwards as they hovered over more trees, and then decided to ascend a little higher to get a clearer view.
"Look! There's the main hillfort to the north!" cried Alyssia.
"That's good, we can get our bearings now," replied Karin.
"Zanadar, have you been here before?" asked Kenny.
"Yes I have, and I do know where people have gone, just further south a little!" he responded, "I wanted you all to figure a bit out to begin with, besides, you've only just asked me now!"
"Let's go, then!" said Kenny.

A few miles south, near a river bank, where there had only been countryside, stood a group of rounded houses.
"It looks like a new age settlement!" cried Alyssia.
"You can see all the vegetables being grown communally," commented Sarah, "and herbs!"
They began to approach, and could see various crafts being done. Tools, wood and materials were evident, and people came and went, busily working.
"They look pretty self-sufficient, Zanadar, is this finally Utopia?" asked Karin.
Zanadar laughed, "yes, it looks as if it is happening at last, and it is much the same over the country. People decided to carry

the stone to where they wanted it, and built directly beside the best resourceful areas, and by fresh ground. All the buildings originally collapsed in many places, or were unfit for use. Is there anything else you need to know?"

"What about transport, governments etc?" asked Kenny, "and is money still used?"

"It was originally, but so many people were tired of the old ways of doing things, and the fact that new buildings had to be put up, and there were less people around, so the survivors decided to get into groups and make their own communities, just as you see it," explained Zanadar, "they eventually dropped all the old ways and are happier for it, and no governments, since there is no money. The people don't need it as they just govern their own affairs!"

"Fantastic! When can we join them?" said Kenny.

"Maybe in another lifetime, my friend!" said Zanadar, his brown eyes radiated a benign glow. "I think we can all return now, don't you?" he said, and everyone agreed.

They hovered back to the exact location from where they started, and walked through into the temple again, for they could see the shimmering interface that linked the two regions, crossing the boundaries of third and fifth dimensions.

"Now sit yourselves down again, for there is another thing for you to consider," instructed Gandar, and he went to a cupboard and extracted a box. He opened the lid, and inside were held several disks, for the Oswestry group could see into it with ease. Indeed, in that rarified atmosphere they were beginning to see what was on that disk already. Gandar held the disk and put it into an edifice near the cupboard, not unlike the devices used on Earth. A glowing emanation came from the machine, and everyone was seeing the same imagery in front of themselves. Gandar let it run for a few minutes until it concluded itself, and then asked what the Oswestry group made of it.

"It looks like an introduction to what lies in the halls of wisdom on this planet," said Kenny.

Gandar nodded, and held up the other two disks he had, "and what is on these two?" he asked.

"I feel they are about the halls of wisdom on Sirius and the Pleiades," answered Alyssia.

"That is correct," he replied, "Anchorin holds copies of the disks from all three caskets, whereas we have many, covering much of the universe. But I would say that wisdom is universal, so those disks differ only very little from all the rest. The only real difference is in how much of it can be perceived and understood!"

"Why did we get introduced to part of the caskets on Astragandara when we could have done so on Atlantis?" asked Sarah.

"Because we want you to know that all is being evoked as it should be, and that the origins for the caskets, civilisations and mankind, all began from elsewhere. With this in mind, you can view the caskets' disks more objectively, without attaching their nature as being earthly in origin, or nature," explained Gandar, "and now you must leave, and return to your homeland. I know you still have many questions, but things will come to you on your journey home, and do not be sad to return to your three dimensional world, for it needs your help, focus on that!"

He smiled warmly, and a golden essence resonated from him, and it radiated throughout the temple, suffusing itself into the Oswestry group, who looked moved once more. Zanadar and the other space beings drew the group towards the exit, and they all departed silently once more.

Once outside, everyone rose up and flew directly back to the hall where the visiting party had all originally arrived on Astragandara. "It has been such a marvellous experience coming to Astragandara," said Sarah, as they all faced Astara, Aurial and Aurastara.

"I'm so glad I could re-experience my homeland," said Alyssia.

"Hope we can all come again!" stated Kenny.

"Thank you so much," added Karin.

They all said goodbye, and boarded the spaceship, but not before Aurastara handed Sarah a large package.

"Remember! That ivy type plant by the waterfall, to help you all adjust to your third dimensional world again."

Sarah smiled broadly, and waved to them as she walked away.

Chapter 12 – The Journey Home

"It's rather nice to have the whole of the Council of Twelve on board," remarked Sarah.
"It somehow feels reassuring, because it is slightly daunting to return to a three-dimensional world, despite Gandar's words of encouragement," replied Kenny.
"Yes indeed," responded Karin, "we should find out more, how the Council of Twelve all cope with inter-dimensional travel."
"I think you won't have to wait long," said Alyssia, "you're attracting their attention already!"
Siral, Maeron and Salaron came over and sat by the Oswestry group.
"There are no secret thoughts in higher dimensions, as you know!" responded Siral, smiling warmly.
"We have the healing rooms, which help us immensely," commented Salaron, "but the best thing to aim for is to ensure that our energy fields are strong, and then it will help to withstand the changes."
"We can do this while at work, and we link to each other, so that we can all focus our healing energy on strengthening each other's energy fields as we go," explained Maeron, "although that is the best method of healing, it is best done in the healing rooms."
"Do you mean that you take it in turns to focus on an individual collectively, in that manner?" asked Kenny.
"Indeed, you have it right!" responded Maeron.
"Can I ask you if we will remember everything once we have returned to the third dimension?" asked Sarah, looking slightly concerned.
"Do not worry, look at us, we are crossing the barriers all the time! You won't forget anything!" replied Maeron, and Sarah looked very relieved.

Everyone watched the displays of light and colour on Astragandara, and as that faded from sight, the beautiful greens of Verdamara became apparent. As those planets receded, the Oswestry group turned their attention away, not wishing to see the pale green light that surrounded all those planets ebbing away to the usual dark skies of the third and fourth dimensions.

The bright light of Sikaron caught the Oswestry group's eyes, and his tall, radiant figure approached them.
"Do not worry about the light fading, and the return to your dimension, you will retain your peace as you go about your

work," he said, reassuringly, "once experienced, never lost, that is how it is for all who visit Astragandara and Verdamara. Now don't forget to take that plant, you'd better begin now!"

"Oh of course!" cried Sarah, "I'd almost forgotten! Come on everyone, let's take some of it."

The group began to chew a couple of leaves, and looked around at the Council of Twelve, and their features seemed more alive since taking the plant. Aurion was standing by Zanadar at the helm, his silvery blue colouring, with bird-like feathers coming from the back of his head, like a crest, and piercing eyes, then Zanadar's benign and jovial mien, with glowing brown eyes and orange-pink skin. Salaron came over to talk to them, and he was also tall and slim, with a faraway look in his eyes. Everyone began to glow brightly, and the Oswestry group looked at each other and knew they were all experiencing the same thing.

Just then, Siral and Maeron hurried over, and indicated for them all to go to the healing rooms.

"It can happen after taking those plant leaves. They can occasionally over-compensate, because the strengths of different batches can vary," explained Siral, "it will wear off shortly a little, but the crystal healing will help to balance it quicker, making it pleasant, rather than cathartic."

"We seem to have spent most of our trip in a dazed state!" laughed Sarah.

"Indeed!" replied Maeron and Siral, smiling genially, "not to worry!"

The crystals lifted the Oswestry group's spirits, and stabilised their energy fields, and after an hour or so, they returned to join the others. As they entered the main control room, Kelaré was there, giving them a drink.

"Come! We are all here dining together, for a three-dimensional realm means we have to get some sustenance too!" he uttered.

The group appreciatively joined in and sat near Kelaré, and Siral and Maeron were nearby.

"I can see you are searching for knowledge of your next step in proceedings," remarked Kelaré, amiably, "perhaps I can help, with my link to the Light Year Command."

"Good! I've been wondering why it is called the Light Year Command instead of the younger planet guidance, for instance," asked Kenny.

"Yes, it is because in this part of our universe, there are huge distances between the youngest planets," replied Kelaré.

"You see," began Maeron, "without wanting to be rude, the youngest planets' inhabitants can be like unruly children that need to be well separated. Some are much worse than Earth, and could be a danger to it if too close, geographically."

"You know that there have been others from slightly more advanced technological cultures that have not been entirely helpful to younger planets," explained Siral, "but in opening up to the universe, these things can occur, but have been, and do get remedied. Sometimes these things are allowed to occur because every young planet needs to understand everything, all aspects of life in your universe, but if the universal Source of good energy is actively called for, then things get remedied."

"You know, it has just come to mind about a vision I had experienced while in Verdamara of lecturing," commented Kenny, "and I saw a chart on the wall behind me, but I couldn't recall what it was, so was it the map of the universe, and do you have one?"

"We are glad you have asked, and yes, we do have a map, you can take one home with you," responded Siral.

"You will understand it well when you see it, and there is some reading matter we can give you that goes with it," said Kelaré, with one of those knowing looks the group recognised so well.

"Kelaré, how long does it take for you to reach Ursa Major from Earth?" asked Alyssia.

"Now there's a question!" responded Kelaré, "I'd say with the docking or landing procedures included, about one hour."

"That's not long!" replied Alyssia, "is it much nearer to Earth?"

"A bit nearer, yes!" responded Kelaré.

"What about to the other eleven planets and star systems?" asked Karin.

"About the same," said Maeron.

Siral smiled gently, "you see, it is the landing and taking off that takes most of the time! The rest is virtually instant!"

Maeron, Kelaré and Siral smiled at the group's reaction, awaiting the response to come next.

"You mean, you can be somewhere almost instantly, once airborne!" cried Kenny.

"How come we are going so slowly?" asked Sarah, looking intrigued.

"The reason is because you all needed to adjust gradually to the higher dimensions," explained Siral, "we can do it easily, but people from third dimension planets, it is not so easy for them."

"Well, thank you for keeping the brakes on all the time!" answered Kenny.

"We just use a form of energy that produces a repulsion, for want of a better word in your language, that links to other planets or substance we pass by, and clings to it somewhat, like throwing out an anchor," replied Siral.

"Could I ask any of you if we may visit Sirius or the Pleiades?" asked Sarah.

Maeron, Siral and Kelaré looked at each other thoughtfully, a moment.

"Well, it could be possible, but only briefly, as we do have work to do, and so have you!" said Maeron.

"Let's ask Aurion and Salaron!" announced Kelaré, and he caught their attention and they came over.

"We shall inform Zanadar to hover over the star systems in question," said Aurion, and he focused his attention on Zanadar.

"We aren't too far away, I shall hasten the ship to the Pleiades first," responded Zanadar, turning to speak to the group from his helm position.

Everyone could see the bright jewels of the Pleiades approaching, with the green light of the fifth dimension surrounding, and the gradual smile emerging on Salaron's face at the thought of an unexpected visit to his home territory.

Soon the craft was hovering over a planet with a royal blue aura, and they soon touched down to a beautiful view of deep blue waters, and hills of a blue-green hue. The Oswestry group accompanied Salaron out of the ship, and walked across the landing area to view a large stretch of countryside to one side, consisting of blue-green grass and many pearl-like flowers. On the other side, a walkway past a decorative fountain, leading to a fairly large building, that looked a bit like a temple to the group.

"Yes, we keep large blocks of the withering plant and blue mist plant in this building, and grow it in these fields," explained Salaron.

"To think what we found came from here, thousands of years ago, and we found it, as if by chance on that beach in Cornwall, inside the casket," remarked Alyssia.

Salaron's eyes lit up as he looked at Alyssia.

"Was it indeed chance? Did the waves have to come to the beach so strongly before you were going to walk there? And so on!" he said.

The group looked at him questioningly.

"But how could the waves do much about it all?" asked Kenny.

"Sometimes we give nature a hand if something needs to occur!" replied Salaron, with that faraway look again.

"So it was all planned, right from the start!" said Kenny, with a curious expression.

"When was the start?" asked Sarah.

"Maybe when we incarnated, or just before," said Alyssia.

"Was it just then or sooner?" asked Salaron.

"Does that mean we have links going right back to Atlantis and Lemuria, and have been returning to try and resolve this?" asked Kenny, looking concerned.

Salaron nodded, "yes, this has been the case, but there have been other individuals involved as well, who have tried to help, but failed for one reason or another. We had all the stops out this time, as you say, and succeeded, with people from Astragandara and Verdamara!" and he smiled broadly.

They all followed Salaron into the building, and could see it was like a library, full of spiritual information.

"I wish we had libraries like this!" exclaimed Sarah.

"Perhaps in time your planet will oblige," responded Salaron.

Salaron took them all to a screen with seats in front, and they sat down, while Salaron put a disk into the side of the screen. The group could see how the Pleiades' life began, much like Earth, with cultures and wars. Again and again, peace was aimed for by the leaders and priests of these cultures and civilisations, but ended up breaking down via warfare and strife once more. Finally, there was a major spiritual breakthrough, and like Sirius, the information said, the peoples of the Pleiades finally began to live in peace and harmony. The CD came to a conclusion and Salaron removed it.

"You know, this is the pattern for all planets. However long the civilisation appears to have continued in that way, of war and strife, things eventually change," he said.

"So Sirius and all other planets have experienced this, and we and other planets of our kind will definitely come to it as well?" queried Kenny.

"Absolutely!" affirmed Salaron, "if people wish and pray for peace often enough, it will occur, you can be certain of that."

"That is very encouraging indeed, despite how things are at present," remarked Alyssia.

"Don't worry!" responded Salaron, "it is sad that people do get so concerned, when there is always a plan in force, as long as they are caring and responsible to the planet, and each other, they personally should not worry, despite how things may look."

Salaron got up from sitting beside the group, and ushered them around the building briefly. The various rooms were occupied by many Pleiadeans, all busy learning or meditating, and there was a beautiful atmosphere of peace.

"I'm going to take you back to the ship now," said Salaron, "as there's much to do, and Sirius is much the same atmosphere, but with a silvery-golden light around things, and of course it produces the other two plants from the caskets, the elixir and amaranth plants, as seeded from Astragandara. Now let's go!"
Before they could board the ship, a large group of beings like Salaron appeared, rushing over towards the group.
"My friends and family," explained Salaron, "they always know what's going on!"
The Oswestry group smiled at the eagerly approaching party, and so they boarded the ship, leaving Salaron for his all too brief reunion.

Once Salaron was on board again, the ship speeded up, and moved along very swiftly.
"There's just enough time for a quick drink!" cried Zanadar, looking towards the group.
They duly helped themselves, watching the screen in front of Zanadar. Only too soon, the familiar sight of Saturn and Jupiter were apparent, swiftly followed by Mars, and then the blue seas and swirling white clouds of Earth. The group could see the large continent of Atlantis, and then they were once again over Anchorin's mountain temple, and being beamed down onto the summit. The group, accompanied by Zanadar, Aurion, Salaron, Siral, Maeron and Kelaré, all met Anchorin in the usual conference room. They all became seated in a semi circular formation, with Anchorin in front. One of the monks came in with a tray of pure spring water for everyone.
"The four of you know quite a bit more now, than before you left, I see!" said Anchorin, with a twinkle in his eyes. "There only remains the viewing of the disks from the caskets, and then you can return home. You will know what to do once you are back."
The group looked at each other in response.
"How long do the disks take to view?" asked Sarah.
"Five minutes each!" replied Anchorin.
"Five minutes!" exclaimed everyone in the Oswestry group, with an astonished look, to which everyone else began laughing.
"It's true! That's all it takes," said Anchorin, still smiling, "I will get the crystals out of the caskets that relate to each of them and their accompanying disks. If you could produce your crystal wands and put them alongside, please. That will ensure relevant information will be stored in your crystals."
On a nearby table, Anchorin put out the caskets, opening the boxes, and took out the disks and main crystals. He put all the

disks by the playing machine, and then indicated for the Oswestry group to put their crystal wands beside the casket crystals. He turned on an ultra violet light under the crystals, and then put the first disk into the slot.
"This is the Atlantean disk," stated Anchorin.
The wall lit up and everyone could see an image of the temple in Chalidocea, and the view scanned to a few streets away, where the Halls of Wisdom were situated. Once inside, the view focused on shelves, and on those shelves were not books but crystals. All the crystals on the table in the conference room lit up at seeing this, and began throbbing strongly. Then the view changed to another one of a library-like setting.

"The first image was of the most recent Halls of Wisdom, contemporary with myself, and this image now, is from the Halls of Wisdom from the period of time when the Northern Island was in existence," commented Anchorin, "and now!" The image changed again to a smaller building of the Halls of Wisdom, which looked very simple in design. Sarah and Alyssia noticed some features that reminded them of Galaron's temple, and quietly remarked on it. Anchorin smiled over to them.
"Yes indeed, it is the Halls of Wisdom from Lemuria," he said.

The crystals on the table from the caskets and the Oswestry group, all glowed and throbbed strongly again. The images on the wall all faded away, and Anchorin gave his full attention to everyone.
"Are there any questions?" he asked, looking around at everyone.
"We were just wondering about the knowledge in the Halls of Wisdom, as all we saw were crystals," explained Sarah, "how will we get to know about it?"
"Will we need to sit with the disks for a while?" asked Alyssia.
"Not at all!" replied Anchorin, "the information has been passed to your crystals, and in a short period of time, things will come into your mind that is illuminating. That is how it works."
"Will there be any Halls of Wisdom in the future?" asked Karin.
"That's an interesting question!" responded Anchorin, "it could happen, if people realised it would be of use, and could intuit the best format for that time period."

Anchorin got up and went to the disk machine, and put another disk into it. A lovely blue-green planet image was visible, and then it focused in on a scene from indoors. It was a view of a huge building, with tall, blue-green beings wandering slowly and

quietly around. There were rooms and corridors lined with shelves, and upon them were crystals. In some of the rooms there were very big crystals, which were glowing constantly, and the ones in Anchorin's conference room were throbbing even more than previously.
"That Hall of Wisdom, one of a number, was partially carved out of the rock, so that those big crystals could be incorporated into the building," commented Anchorin.
"Is it much the same on Sirius?" asked Kenny.
"Well! You will find out shortly," replied Anchorin.
He got up and changed the disk again, and soon enough, the light was shining on the wall. The image zoomed in onto the planet's surface, which was of golds and silvers, like Salaron's description of it. Then a large pyramid came into view, and soon they were inside. The corridors all came from a central point in the heart of the building, radiating out like a star shape, for they each began wide, and narrowed off a bit towards the extremities. The group could now see the plan view for a moment.
"Do you notice anything significant about the interior shape?" asked Anchorin.
"There are four points that terminate in the centre of the pyramid walls, and the other four only converge slightly, and almost look like beams of energy radiating outwards at the pyramid corners," said Kenny.
"Yes," responded Anchorin, "and there is another significant point. Look at the exterior wall!"

The group looked at each other, and then towards Zanadar and the other space beings, the latter only smiled gently, as if in neutral mode, wanting the group to figure it out themselves.
"They look like triangles," said Alyssia.
"..and they are all the same, though some are in mirror image," commented Karin.
"What sort of triangles?" ventured Sarah.
"There are three types," answered Kenny, "equilateral, isosceles and Pythagorean, and these triangles are the latter!"
"Well done!" stated Anchorin, "the Pythagorean triangle is of a proportion that links to sacred geometry, the dimensions of pyramids, and why the proportions of three, four and five?"
The group looked blankly at each other.
"I'm sorry, my maths doesn't go any further than that!" exclaimed Sarah, and there were supportive nods from Alyssia and Karin.

"The secret was truly lost in time, my friends!" exclaimed Anchorin, "it is that the number of three relates to the spiritual body, the number of four relates to the astral body, and the number of five relates to the physical body," explained Anchorin. Everyone still looked puzzled, which made Anchorin chuckle. Zanadar's expression was animated humour, gleaming from his eyes, and the others looked on with gentle smiles.

"I shall explain!" stated Anchorin, "by demonstration!"

He stretched his forefinger out in front of him, and with a fleeting look of concentration, and a beam of light emerged from the end of his finger. He traced the image of a pyramid in three dimensions, between himself and everyone else.

"There! One pyramid!" he announced, "now, here is the square of the hypotenuse," and he drew a square in light, "and let's have that right angled triangle first!" He drew the triangle, attached the hypotenuse on, and then drew the other two squares. "Now, let's relate these shapes to the pyramid, for instance, the base size could be sixty feet, the height would be forty feet, and the sides 57 feet. Now, I will drop them on top of the pyramid, one by one, and then you will see what I mean!"

The hypotenuse went down to the base line.

"You see, I have compared the ratio of the three square's measurements to the pyramid's measurements. The hypotenuse is the base, being the largest of course, the oblique one is the middle sized square, and the height is the smallest. 5,4,3, and the triple energy of the Divine is highest, the fourfold energy of Earthing of the Divine becomes the fourth dimension, and the fifth is manifestation at ground level. It is also related to the five elements, of balance, and is linked to the star of Venus, and to the goddess Isis."

Anchorin paused to allow that information to percolate for the Oswestry group, a moment.

"Do you have any questions about this?" he asked, "and have you considered anything about those lines?"

"Aren't the king's and queen's chambers aligned to these lines?" asked Sarah.

"Correct!" stated Anchorin, "and which is which?"

"The king's chamber is above the queen's!" stated Kenny, and Anchorin nodded his approval.

"How does this relate to the temple on Sirius, and those right angled triangles?" asked Alyssia.

"I had to explain the meaningful dimensions of the pyramid and its relation to sacred geometry, and that is to enable a pyramid to become a place that crosses the boundaries of time and space, since it is truly aligned via the sacred proportions,"

explained Anchorin, "and the right angle is the line of the height from the centre. It is on Sirius that the use of pyramids helped people to transcend those gravitational effects in order to truly link with higher dimensions, wouldn't you agree, Aurion, and everyone else for that matter!" and he smiled warmly.
"Absolutely!" responded Aurion, and the other space beings also stated their agreement.
The group now looked very interested and thoughtful. Anchorin indicated that it was time for them to return back to their own time period.
"If you stay any longer, you won't want to return!" he jested.
"You could be right, there!" responded Kenny.
They all looked at one another in true friendship, and a wordless unity of spirit shone through, recalling their time on Astragandara.

The Oswestry group decided to return home directly from Anchorin's temple, and began to prepare to do so. Zanadar and the other space beings arose from their chairs to leave as well.
"Blessed be, friends!" they all said in unison to the Oswestry group.
"Thank you, and blessed be to you all also," replied the group, also in unison.
Siral produced a few sheets of paper rolled up, and handed them to Kenny.
"The map of our universe, I hadn't forgotten!" he said.
"Lovely! Thank you, Siral," cried Kenny, and he looked at the bundle with almost a look of reverence.
Then Anchorin approached them with a long, thin bundle.
"Open this up when you return. You'll know what to do with it!" he cried.
The group took it, smiled broadly, while holding their crystals, and then vanished back to Oswestry.

Within a shimmer of light in Sarah's well, all four of the group re-appeared in its midst. They swiftly stepped out of it, almost before they materialised and landed, since they knew it would only be comfortable for one person at a time to be standing over the well.
Alendrin and Miara appeared, with an animated look in their eyes.
"Welcome back, everyone!" they cried.
"It's lovely to see you two again, as well," responded Sarah, and the others joined in with their responses.

They all took some of the withering plant, as usual, once at the back door, to reduce to twenty first century size once more, and remove their Atlantean clothes that were now too large for comfort!

"I've forgotten which day it is!" cried Sarah, "when did we leave?"

"It was a Sunday, come to think of it," said Kenny, "since the shop was closed."

"Yes, and we left about mid morning," added Karin, "on 14th July."

"Good! Maybe I can prepare some lunch for us soon, and we can sit down and discuss what we shall do next, once we get sorted out," suggested Sarah.

"A good idea!" responded Alyssia, Kenny and Karin.

Having confirmed they had returned on the same day, via the media, they were able to readjust to being back on home ground again more readily. Once outside in the back garden again, sitting around the table, they began to eat their lunch.

"Let's look at that map of the universe, Kenny!" said Sarah, "I'm extremely intrigued!"

Kenny had a large mouthful of sandwich, and did some quick chewing, while he picked up the sheets from beside his chair.

"Here! See what you can make of it!" he said, "I think we'll need a few more copies!"

He began to peruse the other sheets given to him by Siral. Alyssia and Karin alternately looked at Sarah and Kenny, expectantly. Sarah's expression took on an increasingly curious and amazed demeanour, and naturally, everyone else became intrigued.

"What is going on, Sarah?" they all asked.

"I began to look at this map, and found The Pleiades, Sirius and then Astragandara, and then somehow I was inside the map, traversing the universe itself. It's fantastic!" said Sarah.

"We definitely all need a copy then!" responded Karin, "I'll do a couple for you two and bring them over, either tomorrow or the next day, depending on what needs to be done, chez nous."

"That's perfectly fine, can't wait!" responded Sarah and Alyssia.

"Has anyone brought out that package Anchorin gave us?" asked Sarah.

"Where was it left? I'll get it!" cried Alyssia.

"Actually, I think I took it upstairs when I got changed, and forgot to bring it back outside," replied Sarah, with an apologetic smile.

Alyssia went upstairs and soon reappeared with the package.

"I found it on the landing windowsill. When I was walking downstairs, I distinctly felt we ought to hold a ceremony while opening up this package, everyone!" explained Alyssia.

"We'll go along with that," responded Kenny.

"We can hold the ceremony in the lounge later on," said Sarah, "how about leaving the package by the well for now, just so it picks up the good energy?"

"Sounds good to me," replied Alyssia, and she carefully placed it by the well, and returned to her seat.

Chapter 13 – A New Beginning

Later, when the sun had moved well past the zenith, and the group had done some well-earned relaxing in the sun, as well as helping Sarah tend her herbs and vegetables. This allowed them time to re-integrate to Earthly life once more. A large white cumulus drifted over the sun, casting the whole garden into a muted, shady area, which began to put them into a contemplative mood.

Sarah looked at everyone, "how about that ceremony?" she asked.

Before she had finished, Alyssia was retrieving the parcel by the well, and they all gathered in the lounge a few minutes later.

"Let's contemplate for a few minutes on how the ceremony should go," suggested Sarah.

A few minutes later, they opened their eyes.

"I think we should begin by casting a circle, and then all focus on the parcel," commented Karin.

"Can we not see what this object is?" asked Kenny, pertinently.

"No, we can't at present," replied Sarah, "I know it would be easier just to open it up, but somehow….."

Kenny looked thoughtful a moment, holding his Atlantean crystal, "Yes, you are right, I think we have to know its capacities on an inner level first."

"By looking at it on the subtle levels, we ascertain its characteristics, and are not coloured by its appearance," explained Alyssia.

"Let's make a start!" cried Sarah.

They all focused intently. Candles adorned the central round table, which was the one Sarah had in her lounge in Cornwall, when the casket was first discovered. There were also a number of crystals on it, and a censer with homemade incense drifting out. The long, bound up package lay in the centre of the table.

"A strident energy that directs individuals to find their life path," remarked Kenny.

"A powerful tool for healing, helping with soul loss, and much else in that line," commented Sarah.

"A scrying capacity to understand the nature of life on all planets and star systems," said Karin.

"A tool to help transformation of self and others in a powerful way," exclaimed Alyssia.

They all looked at each other and were then aware that a fifth person was amongst them, with a slightly wry, but humorous expression on his face.
"You are getting close!" he exclaimed.
"Hudlath!" exclaimed Sarah, "when did you arrive?"
"Just a moment ago, I didn't want to intrude on your concentration," replied Hudlath.
"But how did you know we were meditating?" asked Kenny.
"Ah well! I get to know via my crystals!" he replied; "well you'd better open it!" Hudlath pointed at the well-wrapped parcel on the table.
Everyone chuckled a little, and reached for the said item.
"It looks a bit awkward to open," said Karin, "have you got some scissors, Sarah?"
"Yes, I'll get some," responded Sarah, and she got up.
"Sit yourself down, there is a better way to open it, my friends!" announced Hudlath.
They all turned to look at him with mild surprise.
"Focus on surrounding it in strong, white light," said Hudlath, "point your crystals and say after me, 'Bringer of energies that straddle universes, may this structure bear your light and strength, and help to ensure support, and loving energy will be there present for all who work with it. Blessed be,'" said Hudlath.
They all followed suit in repeating the words. To their surprise, the outer covering began to dissolve, leaving an intriguingly shaped object underneath. The group all looked at it curiously.
"What is it?" asked Sarah.
"I can tell you initially what it isn't first!" replied Hudlath, after the initial description. "It has a handle, like for a wand, made of wood and bound around with fabric. Further along, there is a nugget of gold, and then a kind of blade that is convex, and rounded like a cylinder in all angles, but its end tapers to a point," and he looked around at everyone, awaiting their responses.
"Go on!" said Kenny, "what isn't it?"
Hudlath's eyes twinkled animatedly.
"It isn't a wand, or a sword, or even a crystal!" responded Hudlath, "there! That's confused you all, especially judging by your expressions."
"Well you have!" replied Alyssia, "what is it made of?"
"That's a sensible question!" answered Hudlath, "however, will the answer help? It is made of a substance called Relidium, and it holds strong energy within it."
"Relidium makes me think of Reluisia, Hudlath," remarked Karin.

"That's because it has come from there, and the energy?" he enquired.

"Not sure," said Sarah, "since we didn't go there, but I expect the energy was very peaceful and loving."

"Yes, and also very profound, bearing light from the inner planes in the centre of the universe. A strong tool indeed!" explained Hudlath.

He picked it up and held it in his hand, while cradling the blade part with his other palm, then closed his eyes and concentrated. The blade began to illuminate, filling the group with its powerful stillness. They all sat, with a sense of wonder and love in their hearts and minds.

Alyssia could see a mass of golden sparkles radiating from the tool.

'It has an essence of Astragandara,' she thought, and a radiant look permeated her face.

The others noticed her expression and stopped to look at her.

"Alyssia, what is it?" asked Karin.

"Did you not see the golden sparkles coming out of that golden nugget?" questioned Alyssia; "there is some part of it that comes from Astragandara! Look!"

More sparkles emanated, and this time everyone saw them.

"How fascinating!" mused Sarah in wonder.

"Reluisia, and now Astragandara," stated Kenny, "is there a link to Verdamara?"

Hudlath gave Kenny a thoughtful look, and held out the tool to him. Kenny gently took it and examined the blade of Relidium, the nugget of Astragandaran origin, and now the wooden handle, with its fabric cover.

At the end of the handle was a jewel. Kenny looked at it carefully. The jewel began to catch the light, and he could see greenish tints in it. As he looked, he could almost see hints of a green glade in a forest, with bright emerald light shining brightly, and he felt the connection with Verdamara plainly enough. He looked up and nodded to Hudlath, and smiled, and the others understood.

"What does all this tell you?" asked Hudlath.

"It is a tool from the fifth dimension," stated Sarah.

"It is here perhaps to help guide us forwards in our work to be done, while ensuring we don't forget our origins," explained Kenny.

Kenny passed the tool to Karin, and she examined it carefully.

"It is here to keep the energy pure, so we can always remember, and be strong in our work," said Karin.

Alyssia then took the tool and contemplated with it a moment.
"This tool usually is kept in the fifth dimensional spheres, but because of our origins, it has come to us. I think it will be protected, and virtually invisible to most people."
Alyssia paused a moment. "I think it has some deep information to tell us!" she remarked.
"You are doing well, my friends," stated Hudlath, "you have a lot of work to do, but you will be supported by friends!"
The group understood. Hudlath got up to leave, "you must watch the information that those disks put into your wands. Meditate and hold them to your brows, and soon enough they will play back the information, but a lot will just come to you!"
With that he was gone. The group began their meditation, and the crystal wands glowed gently against their brows. They continued for half an hour.

"There are all kinds of wise topics here on these wands. I could see glimpses of teachers in halls of learning, priests in temples, and I knew what they were doing. I felt I could look into their crystals and know just what information they held!" commented Karin.
"Yes, we felt the same thing!" exclaimed the others.
"I think we ought to contemplate all this and write down what we perceive. It might be of use to help us know what our actions will be," said Sarah.
"Yes, a good idea," said Karin.
"How much more of the first book needs to be written?" asked Kenny.
"I'm doing well. With a bit more help, I'm sure I could have it finished in a few weeks time!" stated Alyssia, "though I've still to type it all up!" and Alyssia looked appealingly at Karin.
"We'll all help, Alyssia. Kenny can type as well, you know!" said Karin.
"Yes, we need to get these books out, as I feel they will help our cause," commented Sarah, "perhaps I should begin the second one!"
"I feel I should begin talking about it here and there," said Kenny energetically, "you know, something is stirring!"
"Time to plan and act, everyone!" stated Sarah.

A few days later, the phone rang one morning, and Sarah picked it up.
"Sarah! I've got us a chance to talk about our experience in Atlantis, at a venue that's part conference, part MBS fair!" exclaimed Kenny excitedly.

"How marvellous, where is it happening?" asked Sarah.

"At St Davids!" replied Kenny, "I've provisionally booked it, and if everyone agrees, I'll confirm it today! Do you want to come over and discuss it over lunch?"

"Absolutely, we'll be over pronto. Great!" responded Sarah.

Alyssia came in through the back door into the kitchen, and saw Sarah's excited expression, and asked the reason and Sarah told her.

"Marvellous! Well we've got another hour before lunch, so I'll just finish off a bit more typing, and that will settle book one," remarked Alyssia.

"I've made a lot of notes for book two, just have a look when we return, eh Alyssia," replied Sarah.

Alyssia gave her a thumbs up and went upstairs to conclude her typing work.

"Kenny will be up soon!" said Karin, her face also animated, like the others, in anticipation of this conference opportunity.

Alyssia and Sarah sat down at the kitchen table with Karin; there were salad, bread rolls, and other edibles laid out ready. Kenny briskly came in through the living room door, rubbing his hands together happily.

"Well folks! It's an old friend of mine, Benny, who is running this conference, and he wants us all to talk about our experiences there. I told him that I'm the one geared up more to public speaking, of all our gifts, but as the conference happens in a fortnight's time, it doesn't give us long. Do we have enough material to go with? You have some paintings of Atlantean scenes, don't you Alyssia?"

"Yes, I have a few, about ten that can be framed. Many more, but maybe that's enough for the occasion!" she responded.

"Perhaps a slide show would cut out the framing side, or have both! Sarah, the herbs! We still have our plants, great evidence!" exclaimed Kenny, swiftly, and then he looked at Karin.

"I'm not sure quite what I shall say, I'll just have to meditate on it!" responded Karin.

"Well, that settles it, are we all going for it?" asked Kenny, and a quick affirmation was the response.

"Who will look after the shop?" asked Sarah.

"Glynda has agreed to do her healing, and her boyfriend is happy to serve in the shop and take phone calls from downstairs directly, so that's settled!" stated Kenny.

"Wonderful! Let's enjoy lunch!" said Alyssia, and everyone gave an excited chuckle.

The time went by quickly during those two weeks. Karin managed to bring in many inspired thoughts to talk about, like messages from space beings, thoughts of Viridiana from Verdamara, and also information from the wands. Amongst all the preparations, the first book was finalised, and the second one well on its way, with the help of the others, and even précis thoughts for the third book were in place. Alyssia got a slide show into operation, and the allotted time drew very close.
The next day, Sarah and Alyssia arose quite early, and set off after a prompt breakfast, to go around to Kenny and Karin's with their luggage, then they would all travel down to St Davids together.
"Don't forget the crystals and our clothing!" said Sarah.
"All packed!" responded Alyssia, "and ready to go!"
"Good!" replied Sarah, rushing to the front door with her belongings.

Once at the flat, they went upstairs. Kenny was organising the plants towards the flat door.
"It's all right girls, we won't take the huge ones! Just these little offshoots!" said Kenny.
"Yes, but they don't stay tiny for long!" remarked Sarah.
"Oh well, it will cause some drama!" said Kenny, gaily; "we may have to leave them at Benny's if necessary, till I can get them later."
Karin cheerfully greeted them, and took a pile of luggage to her car, and then Kenny took the plants and a few bits of food.
"Don't need too much, food's on the house!" he mentioned in passing, to Sarah and Alyssia, and they responded favourably. They picked up some items and took them to the car also.
"Anything more upstairs?" asked Karin.
Kenny paused, "I don't think so, unless you fancy a few more of those boxes!"
"He's talking about a load of biscuits I got from a store, one of his favourites!" explained Karin, laughing.
"Ok, just our stuff to grab, and then we can go," stated Sarah.

"It's a bit of a squeeze with all our bags, as well as the Atlantean gadgetry!" cried Sarah, adjusting herself in the back seat.
"I've got a roof top box in the store, I'll just get it!" responded Kenny, and he went to rummage inside a doorway, adjacent to the flat and shop exit. He returned and attached it onto the

roof, and proceeded to fill it with the excess luggage that was inside the seating area.
"That's better!" he exclaimed, "let's go!"
Everyone smiled happily with relief, due to reclaiming the extra space, and that they could begin the journey.
"We'll just go down the A483 for a while, eh!" said Kenny.
"Yes, that's right, then cut across from Newtown via Langurig," replied Karin, "then head to Aberystwyth."
"Lovely!" exclaimed Alyssia, "it's a beautiful day for travelling down the coast."

The journey went smoothly with a break at Aberystwyth for a brisk trudge over the sands for ten minutes. Once at St Davids, Benny greeted them jovially, and escorted them to their rooms, which were tastefully decorated in pale lilac, peach and golden shades.
"Make yourselves at home," said Benny, who was a tall, stocky man, with dark hair and a slight beard, "lunch is on shortly."
"Thanks Benny!" responded Kenny, and then, turning to the others, "I'm down for an intro to our work this afternoon, and then all properly tomorrow!"
"I can begin to put my work up," commented Alyssia, "I'll see whether I can be speedy enough after lunch!"
"So you will, if we all help!" responded Sarah.
Alyssia laughed and put her arm around Sarah.

"You know, I hadn't even stopped to fully consider what the response would be to seeing our Atlantean clothes, crystals and plants," commented Sarah, "after all, how many twelve foot high people do you see!"
"That's true, it's strange how ordinary it is to us, I never thought how odd it's going to appear!" replied Karin.
"Should we just see how the initial response is, and then keep the rest under wraps until people get acquainted with it all?" queried Alyssia. "I know we have talked about this before we came, but somehow, now we are faced with an audience, and we'd been so busy with those books to give it all our thought."
"We've come here because Benny said there would be people coming, who are open to this kind of thing," informed Kenny, "they are shamans, healers, journey workers, past life therapists, who are all open to time travelling."
"I just hope they are open minded enough!" responded Sarah.
"There! That looks good!" exclaimed Alyssia.
She took a step backwards to admire the collection of pictures of hers everyone had been putting up in the conference hall.

"Exquisite indeed!" announced Kenny.
"I wouldn't have managed without your help, as that lunch was really so lovely, I couldn't help eating more than standard requirements," said Alyssia.
"The standard requirements for superlative cooking always exceed the standard requirements of standard cooking," replied Sarah, chuckling.
Benny appeared a moment later, "Hello all! Ah, what lovely paintings! I shall be examining them later on. Are you all ready? Is it just Kenny speaking this afternoon?"
"Yes, that was intended, but I may ask for a brief summary from the others if the spirit moves me!" replied Kenny.
"Well, I like a few surprises, and I'm sure you all have a few up your sleeves!" laughed Benny. "I shall ask everyone to come through now. You'll be third in line, ok!"
"You're on, friend!" responded Kenny, and Benny gave him a pat on the shoulder and strode off.
The Oswestry group found some seats to one side of the hall, as a large crowd of people began to enter the room. Benny followed them in, once they had more or less found their seats, and began to anticipate what Benny would say.
"Good afternoon, everyone, glad to have you here. This is a special conference this weekend, focusing on time travel, and entering different dimensions. I know many of you, and have been privileged to discover the work you do, and we shall be sharing this knowledge together over the weekend. This afternoon, as you know, each individual or group shall be sharing a quick peek, like a précis, so we can have a taste of what's to come over the next two days. There are those of you who intend to stay on for the full week, so we can go in depth during that time. Now! Without further patter from me, I shall invite the first speaker to come forward."
Benny went to sit down on the other side by his wife, who had just entered quietly. The first speaker walked upto the dais and began.
"My name is Gareth Green, and I am a shamanic healer and have done much inner journeying work. I work with groups, and see their interconnecting lines that link them and their social groups together, and I help them to understand how they can solve problems caused by those links, when in time they occurred, and what will happen to them once they are removed. I can also tell the type of terrain that suits people best, that is, the best places for them for healing and quality of life, or where their destiny will be best worked out. It is not quite time travel like the film, 'the time machine', but I can scan time periods to

see how things are going to help people. I can also see into the people's future a little to help there also."

The man gave an example of someone's problems who didn't mind being discussed, and then concluded his talk.

The next person came forward, who was very much interested in UFO's, and had channelled a lot, and also given many talks around the country, explaining about how the UFO's could come and go between one time period and another, and from one dimension to another, and that he'd seen a number of them. His name was Reg Caldwell.

Now it was the Oswestry group's turn. Kenny rose and strode over to the dais, brought forward a little table to put the Atlantean wands on it.

"My name is Kenny, one of a group of four, seen over there, and they will introduce themselves briefly." He indicated the group with a sweep of his hand.

"We have all had a dramatic journey, which has taken up the last few years of our lives. Really, it was a series of journeys, which comprise such meaning for us all. We journeyed to Atlantis, and met high priests in their temples, also to Lemuria, and to other planets. It all began with a casket washed up on a Cornish beach, which contained a group of crystals and some seeds. You may find this unbelievable that crystals could take anyone back to Atlantis, however, these ones did, and although we don't have those crystals or the casket any more because they needed to stay in Atlantis, we were given some other crystal wands by the high priest of the mountain temple, who is called Anchorin, and they are here on this table."

Kenny went over to pick up his crystal wand, and held it up to show the audience.

"We have used these wands ever since for time travel! I also wish to say that Anchorin was one of a number of high priests we met in their Golden Age time periods, about 12,000 years BC. They are all telepathic, and when we visited, they took us to their temples of healing, and we had become telepathic by the time we returned home!"

Kenny beckoned Karin over, and she approached, picking up her wand from the table.

"I am Kenny's partner, and in-between journeys we run a new age shop called Plas Myrddin. My part in this conference talk is to give messages from the people we have encountered, from Atlantis, Lemuria, from the space beings we travelled with, and from the beings on the planets we visited," explained Karin.

She then left the dais with her crystal, and Kenny beckoned Alyssia, who in turn, picked up her crystal and approached.

"I am the clairvoyant and artistic member of the group, and you will be able to view some of my paintings that are hanging in this room. They are scenes we all encountered on our travels, and I have many more images that will be shown over the weekend. For instance, one shows the lovely mountain temple of Anchorin, another the Garden of Eden on Atlantis, the crystal valley on Lemuria, where Sarah and I gained insights, and much more! It is now Sarah's turn!"

Alyssia left and Sarah approached, taking her crystal.

"I am the one who is keen on herbs, and there have been some very interesting herbs used in our journeys, and that will be talked about tomorrow. But ponder on Alice in Wonderland's edibles, for she had to change size, and you have a clue!"

Sarah gave a knowing smile and departed.

"We shall stop now and leave you with some intriguing thoughts to ponder on!" concluded Kenny.

He smiled broadly and left the dais.

The audience had been very quiet and now looked very interested, and there were a number of excited murmurs rippling around the room. Benny swiftly rose and came to the dais again.

"Now, there is another group who wish to talk about healing methods, and then we will have a short break. Okay everyone, you will be able to find things out over the weekend," instructed Benny, and all who had been talking began to quieten.

The break arrived, and the Oswestry group got up to take a stroll outside for a few minutes.

"I think we are going to cause a bit of a stir here!" said Sarah.

"Yes, now that it is here, I'm not sure anyone else has actually travelled back in time the way we have, nor the future," commented Alyssia.

"You have an interesting story to tell," came a voice from behind the group, "I am a publisher of all kinds of stories, including some mind, body and spirit, and I am on the look out for something different, and you all certainly have something intriguing to offer. Have you thought of writing anything about your experiences?"

"That's a coincidence," cried Kenny, now facing the man, as were all the others, "we are writing the books up now, it will be a trilogy, and we've finished the first book!"

"I'd really like to see it, here's my card," he replied emphatically, and was about to depart, but Alyssia spoke.
"I hope that the storyline would be followed fairly well, and nothing changed too much, I hope," said Alyssia, "is that fair to ask?"
"Yes, fair enough, and if all looks good, I would ensure that nothing out of the ordinary would be added, just for the sake of it!" he responded, reassuringly. He then smiled and departed.
"There! What good timing!" commented Sarah.
"Indeed!" chorused the others.
They all went back into the hall to listen to the other contributors for the rest of the afternoon.

Later on, they were talking to Benny in his private room.
"I still find it hard to acknowledge that you've been to Atlantis, just as we are now, simply using a crystal each," said Benny, his hand on his head a moment, looking thoughtful, but an expression of puzzlement was not far away. "Can you give some proof to the audience, perhaps?"
"We will have to consider the options, Benny, how about some Atlantean plants and what they do?" suggested Kenny.
"What do they do?" asked Benny.
"They help sustain a person, make them Atlantean sized, make them disappear and reduce them to Earthly size. Those are the four options!" stated Kenny, "how about that? We could take less herbs, and not become full sized, which is twelve feet high!"
"Oh yes, I think full size would be quite a shock!" responded Benny, "could you demo it for me here, so I can see how it will look?"
"Certainly Benny," replied Kenny, "there's nothing too shocking about it to us, it's become so natural. Shall we get some of the equipment now? Maybe just one of us can demonstrate?"
"I don't mind, I'm the smallest anyway!" responded Sarah, and she was off to obtain her belongings.

On return, she picked the Atlantean outfit from her bag, and put it on. She reached for her tinctures of elixir and withering plant.
"This garb always looks wrinkled and un-exotic before we get bigger," stated Sarah, "I shall take a small amount of the elixir plant, just to show a slight amount of growth."
Sarah took a sip and immediately grew by a few inches, and Benny looked intrigued.
"Now I shall take some more," said Sarah, and she rose another few inches in height. She repeated this twice more, until she was about seven feet and nine inches in height.

"This is more child sized, but it shows sufficient growth to prove the point that the plants work, and there's nothing like it on planet Earth today," commented Sarah, "I shall use some of the withering plant tincture to shrink back to size once more."
Sarah duly drank the liquid, and gradually reverted back to her original size. Benny sat looking amazed, and was lost for words.
"I'm very impressed, and think it will work," said Benny, at last. "By the way, did you know we are having a musical evening, with various stalls, some with products by the participators. The music is designed to enhance energetic levels, they say!" said Benny jovially.
The next day saw everyone gathered in the conference hall again.
"I see by the wall chart that we will be third again after Gareth and Reg, like yesterday!" commented Kenny, "then that healing group after us."
"It's going to be a busy weekend!" responded Sarah.
"Let's get some breakfast folks, it's ready!" announced Alyssia, for she and Karin had just quickly gone to the dining room door.
"Coming right up!" cried Kenny and Sarah.
They collected their cereals, juices and hot drinks and found a convenient space.
"Oh look, it's Gareth!" said Kenny, "hello there!"
"Good morning all!" responded Gareth, "I'm looking forward to hearing more about your Atlantean experiences. It sounds most intriguing!"
"Well thank you, we'll tell all in the slot, and how it started," explained Kenny.
"Yes, we are writing the whole experience up, as so much has happened, we could be talking all week long, I'd say!" explained Alyssia.
"A book, lovely!" responded Gareth, "I'll give you my contact details. Do let me know when it will be published."
"We will indeed!" replied Kenny, "and my secretary here will give you our contact details," and he put his hand on Karin's shoulder.
"That's right, I'm the organised one here!" laughed Karin.

Kenny strode onto the dais and introduced the sequence of events during their presentation. He gave a brief outline and then continued with some of his own experiences.
"I was given the task of gatekeeper at various times, when there were occasions initially in our experiences of Atlantis, when the darker elements came in. This was due to the three caskets being mislaid. Once they were returned to Anchorin's temple,

things improved dramatically. Nature spirits from Atlantis joined us on many occasions too, which takes us to the first part of our presentation given by Alyssia. She will show many images of paintings done of our journey, and includes images of the people there."

Kenny turned on his heel and looked at Alyssia, who was bringing over the equipment, and put it on the table. Benny had put up a whiteboard behind the table beforehand, and so Kenny linked it with the laptop.

"Hello! I have here quite a lot of images, many are just sketches and not reached the painted stage, but I brought them due to their informative value," she explained.

Alyssia clicked until she arrived at an image of the casket.

"Here, this is what it looked like, with the crystals on top. We chanted notes that resonated to them. We stood in a circle, repeating the chant until the casket opened and we could see the crystals inside. Next to it are images of the original crystals we had. We three women discovered we had been high priestesses in Atlantis, and our task was to help return the caskets, and much else. Here is our first view of Atlantis, the coastline, and then how it looked when we landed at the main city, Chalidocea. Here is a sketch of the main temple there, and another image of the temple in the clouds, the one belonging to Anchorin. Now I have here an image of Anchorin, and another high priest who visited us in Oswestry called Hudlath. He also lived in Atlantis two hundred years after Anchorin."

Alyssia continued to scroll through the images, explaining about their content, then another image came up, and she paused for a moment.

"This is a special place on Atlantis, the Garden of Eden, and was looked after by three high priestesses, who hold the energy of the land within their temple, and tend it carefully. This is the entrance gate, guarded by Arwena, and here are the three high priestesses and goddesses, Anui, Deanu and Giana. The other images on the walls are of the temple in the Garden of Eden on Verdamara, a planet we visited, and another one on Astragandara, and was the last one we went to, taken there by the space beings, of which I have sketches here to show you."

Alyssia picked out images of Zanadar, Siral, Aurion and Salaron, and then a rough one of all the Council of Twelve. She then concluded and went to sit down again. Sarah then approached.

"Sarah specialises in herbs, and will talk about the herbs we used that came out of the casket we found," said Kenny.

Sarah clicked on a different file on the laptop and accessed some images.

"I wish to show you some images of the amazing plants we have, which were grown from the seeds we found in the casket. You know, we never thought they'd grow after all that time, but, hey presto, up they came once put in some compost. I sprinkled on some green powder found in the casket, and to everyone's amazement, they grew up to the ceiling in a day, and were exploding seed pods all over the living room, and Kenny and Karin's bedroom.

Here's an image of the elixir plant seed, it's a big spiky seed, and is used to make us expand to Atlantean size! The next is a delicate one called blue mist plant, and is used to make us disappear if required, because at times we needed to stay safe. The third is called amaranth and is a food substance, and is quite an important requirement in the Atlantean diet. The fourth is the withering plant, and the name is due to shrinking us back to normal present day size.

I know you may think this is all sci-fi stuff, so we are going to give you a demonstration of size change near the end of our session.

I saw these plants and others, growing in the main temple grounds in Chalidocea, and others in other places on our travels. I think that is enough for now, so will stop and hand you back to Kenny," concluded Sarah.

"Now we have Karin, who has begun to channel messages from various beings, and has some ready to read to you," explained Kenny.

"Hello, I have a few readings I channelled over the last week, and if there's enough time, I shall channel something for you. The first is from the space beings, the Council of Twelve who we travelled with.

'My friends, and friends at large, we invite you to look upwards to the starry realms and see beyond one sphere to the spheres of infinite vastness, and the glory found there. We do our work to help third dimensional planets to rise towards higher ones, and are happy to be supportive to all. Link to the Divine Source of the Infinite, and all will unfold well.'

The next message is from a being called Viridiana, who lived on the planet Verdamara, and escorted us all around while we stayed. I was able to channel a message from her despite the distance, via my crystal.

'Eons apart, yet not so! Our green planet holds a key of significance that will help your planet. Look now into your crystal and you will see what it is!'

Of course I wondered what it was, and so I linked to the crystal and saw an image of a diamond emanating green light, and I saw that shaft of light growing brighter and coming into Earth and being sustained by it.

Another message was from the Garden of Eden on Atlantis.

'We speak as one, and know this, that we are planetary guardians from Earth's past, yet we still exist, and still aid her even now, somehow. Draw near and see how we bring these energies into Mother Earth, and we can share our gifts with you!' Now I wish to channel another message for you. I shall ponder a moment to see what comes."

Karin picked up her crystal that was on the table by the laptop inside a cover, which she removed.

"This message is from one of the nature spirits, who joined us when we went on our travels, a fairy called Leannah."

'I greet you from Pistyll Rhaeadr, and wish you to know that we can see all the efforts made by everyone who works for the good of all, and it is much appreciated, and us nature spirits warm to you, and spurs us on to ensure Mother Earth is cared for to the best of our ability, and we send our energy to man, to help you all bring about harmony and peace in the world. Blessed be, Leannah.'

"Well, that rounds up my section of the talk," concluded Karin, and she smiled to the audience.

Then Sarah and Alyssia joined Karin with their Atlantean clothing and equipment, and handed over the same to Kenny and Karin.

"Now everyone, we are going to conclude with the pièce de resistance! This is where we show how we expand to fit our clothing, and we use the elixir plant to do this," he explained.

They took a few steps away from the edge of the dais, and changed their clothing behind a screen. They returned shortly, gathering on the dais again, with crystals in one hand, and their individual phials of elixir tincture in the other.

"We shall take one sip to begin with, and show how we grow, gradually, and then take some more," explained Kenny.

They sipped and began to get larger. There were a few gasps from the audience. Then took some more and grew again, and continued with the process until they were seven and a half feet tall.

"We could continue until we reached twelve feet, but Benny's ceiling is too low, though maybe this proves the point. We would then link to our crystals and disappear to another time zone, but we feel we have done enough for now. Besides, our time is up now!" commented Kenny, "and we have to return to normal height too. This is done using the withering plant tincture."

"Oh, the bottles are by our chairs, I'll get them!" cried Sarah, "just a few sips, about the same amount, and back to normal!"

They concluded matters, gave a polite bow, and then walked back to their seats. There was a sudden eruption of tumultuous applause from everyone in the audience, which made the Oswestry group turn to look in surprise, and then they all smiled and thanked them.
The weekend went well, and everyone's talks were interesting, and many contact details exchanged. One or two were people who were therapists, but also ran conferences and events themselves. The Oswestry group were now suddenly in demand!

The last day of the weekend, Sunday, saw everyone gathered for a questions and answers session, where anything over the weekend could be questioned about further.
"Would it be possible to see the Oswestry group disappear to another time zone, or even one of their associates invited to come through, just to prove one hundred per cent that it is really in existence," said a therapist, thoughtfully, "I don't want to put you under undue pressure, only if it could be possible."
Benny was convening the debate, and looked towards Kenny and asked, "would it be possible?"
"I think we'd have to ask Anchorin first, if you don't mind me going off in private for a moment, and giving an answer shortly," commented Kenny.
"Ok Kenny, that would be fine, I'm sure," then Benny looked at the therapist, who said it was perfectly fine.
Kenny went off through a nearby door, and up to their room, held his crystal and focused on 12,000 BC, and Anchorin. The familiar image of Anchorin appeared.
"Hello Kenny, how are things?" asked Anchorin.
"All is well, we have given a talk on Atlantis etc., and all has had a very favourable response, but during the debate at the end, someone asked if one of the Atlanteans could appear to everyone. I am not keen on novelty or curiosity experiences, but they are genuine people, and I wondered if something could happen, just to bring home this time travel business," explained Kenny.
"We could send Jadeir, he wouldn't mind. I'm not sure about Hudlath, but I'm very busy at present. I'm sorry I can't come," replied Anchorin, "I shall get them to contact you, either or both, whoever is willing."

Anchorin's face faded, and Kenny waited for a response to come shortly. After a few minutes there was a signal and Hudlath's image became visible.

"Now! I hear you want to do a conjuring trick, is that it?" asked Hudlath, with his usual wry expression, and an animated look in his eyes.

"If you don't mind, the talk of ours went down very well, and we even expanded ourselves to a certain height as well! So, it would be safe, and the organiser Benny, would ensure confidentiality, I'm sure," explained Kenny, earnestly.

"I think it may be safe enough! Better by far than some of our escapades, I'd say! Well! I'll appear in my green attire! How will that do? When?" asked Hudlath.

"Oh, fairly soon, shall I set a time and I'm sure that will be fine. Say fifteen minutes!" stated Kenny, "by the way, the hotel is in St Davids, south west Wales, and it's called Bay View Hotel."

Hudlath gave a little smile and disappeared.

Kenny returned to the conference room and went over to Benny to explain the latest.

"Our friend Kenny says someone will appear in nearly fifteen minutes," said Benny.

An excited murmur ran through the audience. Kenny's wand glowed and he held it up. Hudlath's face was visible again.

"I'm just checking where exactly I'm to appear; yes, I've got my bearings exactly now!" said Hudlath, and he disappeared again.

Benny noticed what had happened by revealing a curious glance, but the audience were too busy asking another question from one of the talks to notice.

As the fifteen minutes were about to expire, Kenny went over to Benny and brought it to his notice.

"Right everyone!" said Benny, "the magic moment has arrived. I think I will step to one side to ensure the person has plenty of space."

Kenny had done the same. Amidst the silence, Hudlath in his green velvet jacket appeared on the dais. Many people just stared with open mouths.

"Greetings everyone! You can close your mouths now!" announced Hudlath, with a slight grin. "I am Hudlath from Atlantis, and I am a high priest from 11,800 BC. Is there anything anyone wishes to know?" he asked.

"How can you speak our language so well, when the civilisation you come from is so long ago?" asked one woman.

"Ah! I've travelled about very frequently, that is why. I can fit into many time periods!" replied Hudlath.
"Could any of us go back to see what it was like?" asked another.
"You would have to have a serious reason for returning, or else it would be disruptive to various time periods to have lots of vagrant people popping in. The trouble is, if you say yes to one, many others give their reasons for going, and it could get difficult. I think the best thing would be to show you a keyhole view of a bit of Atlantis via the crystal. If you would like to queue up, a row at a time, I could let you see," said Hudlath, "is that fine?" he asked Benny, who agreed.
Hudlath prepared to contact a priest on the outskirts of Chalidocea, explaining why he was in contact. Then he began to usher everyone over.
"This is a view of the main city, Chalidocea, with the temple, streets and houses. Very picturesque!" he announced.
The people all thronged close behind each other, eager to see. After everyone had seen, the image vanished, and then so did Hudlath, very suddenly, with a wave and a wry smile.

Later on, Kenny and the others were talking to Benny again, and his wife was coming and going, preparing some cakes and pies ready for break time. She would periodically peer through into the lounge, with a sunny smile on her face, asking if anyone wanted a cuppa.
"You met a publisher did you say?" queried Benny, a little astonished, "I don't recall one coming here! Did you see him today?"
"No, I didn't, actually," replied Kenny, "I meant to ask you yesterday, but strangely, the thought went out of my head. Focusing on our talk instead!"
"I wonder where he found out about this conference?" queried Sarah.
Kenny revealed the business card, and showed it to Benny.
"John P. Caldecott, Pontcanna Publishers, Cathedral Square, Llandaff. I think I'll ring him to find out how he knew!" said Benny, emphatically. "I'll do it on Monday and let you know. I also have contacts in Cardiff who could check him out."
"Thanks Benny. I guess we'll have to think about returning back to base camp, eh folks?" commented Kenny, "it's been great here!"
"Yes, it's been a very interesting weekend, thank you," responded Sarah.

The others showed their appreciation, and stirred to get their belongings and leave.

The next day, Benny contacted in the evening to say that the publisher was genuine, and the man had felt a strong intuition to visit St Davids, and since he liked the area a lot, he decided to stay for a night.
"That's excellent, Benny!" exclaimed Kenny, happily, "we can send the first book's chapters off to him, pronto!"
Sarah and Alyssia were in the flat, helping Karin by preparing a meal, while she went to look over what Glynda and her partner had done over the weekend, in the notes they'd left.
"We can go ahead, folks!" said Kenny.
"I'll print out the first three chapters tomorrow," responded Alyssia.
"I don't mind doing that if you want me to post it," said Karin, "I've got plenty of paper, envelopes and stamps!"
"Well, thank you, that would be good!" replied Alyssia.
"You know, we've had a couple of messages already, asking if we'll do more talks," exclaimed Kenny.
"Whereabouts?" asked Karin.
"In Chester and Glastonbury," he replied.

Over the next few weeks, the publisher had accepted the manuscript in total, and was going ahead with publication. The group had been to Chester to give the talk there, and were about to finalise arrangements for their visit to Glastonbury. There was a knock at the door and Sarah opened it.
"Oh Annie! Nice to see you, come in!" exclaimed Sarah, cheerfully.
"Are you busy? I've not seen you for a while," asked Annie.
"Yes, in a word!" replied Sarah, "we've been giving talks about our travels. Our books are going to be published, and we're about to go to Glastonbury for another talk!"
"Is there anything I can do, Sarah?" asked Annie.
"I think it's high time we told you everything we've done so far," responded Sarah, "as we're always so busy with all this. You see, we don't know how things will work out, whether all the talks will be favourable, I will explain about the wands and our expansion to Atlantean size, etc."
They went into the lounge, having obtained a drink, and Sarah explained in detail.

"We had wished we could have taken you to Atlantis, but we were advised to not bring any visitors at this stage," explained

Sarah, "mainly because the tasks we had to achieve were allotted to us."

"It's fascinating, Sarah!" exclaimed Annie, "you know, I've longed to know more about Atlantis."

"Have you seen the well before?" asked Sarah, "and met our residents there?"

"Well, I have in fact," replied Annie, "one day I called at the door, and you were out. An elf and fairy came around the corner and said 'have you seen the well?' and they took me over and showed me the inscriptions on it, the codes that Alyssia had seen, and how it's a magical portal to Atlantis and beyond. They also asked it I'd like to travel there, of course I said yes! They smiled and said perhaps I'd be able to go some day."

"Interesting! Maybe things will come clearer on that matter soon," replied Sarah, and she paused for reflection a moment. "I think it will be a good idea if I gave you some of the tinctures we use for travelling to Atlantis, and will give you some instructions with them, is that ok?"

"How wonderful!" responded Annie, "will I need a crystal?"

"Yes, but you'll be provided for when necessary," replied Sarah.

Chapter 14 – The Seeds of Amaranth

"Glynda and her partner Garry want to buy our business!" said Kenny excitedly, "that would free us up no end!"
"But where would you live?" asked Sarah.
"We would stay in the flat until we find something else," responded Kenny, "maybe get a camper van!"
"Ho! However, I feel it's the right thing to do," said Sarah, thoughtfully, "this freeing ourselves up. You know, I've felt the need to move too, but I still love it here, and the well would have to be covered again."
"To be honest, Glynda said they had another couple of friends who wanted to join them at some point, and I told them about your house!" said Kenny.
"You didn't!" responded Sarah, surprised. "So, I've got to get a camper van too, eh!"
Kenny laughed, "how about it?"
"I don't know, the talks won't sustain us that much, will they, and the books haven't been published yet!" stated Sarah.
"There's no rush, as the couple live at a commutable distance," he replied.
"Is it in two days time we go to Glastonbury, Kenny?" asked Sarah, "I've been so busy with apple picking etc., in the garden, I realised I hadn't put it on the calendar."
"Indeed, start packing!" he replied.
They said goodbye to each other and put their phones down.

Some weeks later, the group had even more invites to various talks around the country. Kenny and Karin had found a chalet over in the campsite at Pistyll Rhaeadr.
"Sarah! There's another chalet available, I think it is right for you to come here too!" Insisted Kenny, over the phone, "we need to be free of ties in what we do now."
"You're probably right, but the well?" questioned Sarah.
"Go and ask Alendrin and Miara," insisted Kenny, "you know, it's strange, but I've felt the presence of Jadeir and Hudlath across the barriers of time, somehow insisting on changes, these changes. I'm not entirely sure why, but the well spirits may help us to know."
"Ok, I'll do it now, and then consider the next step to take, Kenny," said Sarah, firmly.

She put down the phone and walked resolutely outside into the back garden. The place she had grown to love dearly. She walked gradually over to the well, as if she was savouring the presence of this moment, as with all the experiences here over the past year or two as they flashed through her mind. The links to Atlantis, Lemuria, the starways, and Sirius. Did they really have to leave the well behind? Just then, Alendrin and Miara appeared.

"Do not doubt, Sarah. It is time for you to consider the next stage. The well has done its work. It will always be sacred, and a link to other realms, but only if the house owners are to work with it. Fortunately, the next owners will learn, and are open to this, so Annie can teach them," said Alendrin.

"Oh good! I feel reassured knowing that," replied Sarah, and her serious expression relaxed into a sunny smile, "knowing that, I feel I can release this place, as I had felt I was a guardian."

"We know," responded Miara, gently, "and could see you would have stayed for the rest of your life. Now you are free, so tell your friends to come and buy the property."

Sarah gave a small laugh, "I shall, and will tell Alyssia too, and I know she will be pleased!"

Sarah turned to walk back to the house, and she smiled at Alendrin and Miara, who both smiled back, and disappeared again.

Later that night, Alyssia returned from a trip, and she and Sarah were sitting on the sofa together.

"Oh, that sounds just right, are they coming tomorrow?" asked Alyssia.

"Indeed, it shouldn't take long to organise if they want to buy it. I've informed the camp site we'll be over for a look at the other chalet too," replied Sarah.

"Well organised!" responded Alyssia, "by the way, my day was lovely!"

"Oh yes, of course," cried Sarah, "where did you get to after all?"

"I felt inspired to just visit the sacred places around us, and take sketches at each, depicting the energies there and how they all link in together. The only one I didn't do was Pistyll Rhaeadr!" said Alyssia, and she smiled broadly.

"Don't need to when we're going to live there, eh!" responded Sarah, "would you help me decide what we'll take with us, tomorrow?"

"I certainly will, Sarah," replied Alyssia.

Some weeks later, Sarah and Alyssia were leaning on the balcony of their chalet, looking down the narrow valley that was bathed in the early morning light.

"We are incredibly fortunate living here, aren't we, Sarah," said Alyssia, marvelling at the scenery.
"Absolutely, my friend," replied Sarah, "that Glastonbury trip was most fortunate too."
"Yes, we had such a positive response," agreed Alyssia.
They could picture the rooms in the healing centre, past which a corridor took them to a large room full of chairs and a willing audience. The format they had used in St Davids was repeated again, and received enthusiastically, and they were asked to return on several more occasions.
"We now have two more talks in London area, and then one in Birmingham," Kenny had said on return to Pistyll Rhaeadr.

The group had already been to London, and were due to go to Birmingham the next week.
So the weeks passed, giving the talks. There seemed to always be a demand for them. Finally, the first book was published, and there was a talk as usual, given in Cardiff, and a book signing to follow. The press got word of it and came to investigate.
'Travellers in time intrigue – links to Atlantis' was the headline. 'First book published, hot seller.' The publisher was over the moon, congratulating the group and started talking of film rights.
"As long as the context of the book is adhered to, and no other characters put in that don't exist, then we would allow it, otherwise no!" the group had insisted.

One morning Annie appeared at the chalets.
"Good morning all! I want to tell you something really interesting," she cried.
"Come inside Annie," responded Sarah, "come and tell us!"
They all went into Kenny and Karin's chalet, and managed to find enough seats for everyone.
"Four is okay, five is a bit of a squash I'm afraid," said Kenny, apologetically, "but we're all agog!" and he smiled jovially.
"You see, I've been looking after those intriguing plants of yours," explained Annie, "they are getting huge, and I felt I needed to find other people who could take some. Just with that thought, a seed of amaranth fell off in front of me. It was kind of strange, but as I picked it up, an image went through my mind to grind it up and make a paste, and apply it to wounds, sprains or painful joints, and to share it with others, maybe sell it. What do you think?" she enquired, "there may be other uses, besides."

"That's a good point, Annie," remarked Kenny, "a sound legacy to offer to the world, if they prefer that to our story."
"Yes, it may be another aspect that will enhance our cause," responded Sarah.
"I wonder what else it may be good for?" mused Alyssia, "why don't we make up a batch and try it out for ourselves and see!" suggested Karin.
"But I wonder why it should have different properties, because it is a paste, instead of a tincture," remarked Sarah.
"Don't know, let's find out!" said Kenny.
"Wouldn't your new neighbours or Glynda take the new plants?" queried Alyssia.
"What are the new people like, have you met them yet, Annie?" asked Karin.
"Yes, I did see the couple looking around the garden, and they looked gentle and kind, and strangely, it was as if the plants were telling me they could live there. It sounds strange, but they were telling me all about Atlantis. It was not verbal, but by impressions and flashes of images," explained Annie, looking a bit uncertain.
"How wonderful that you have such an affinity with the plants, Annie," cried Sarah, "I have had such things happen for myself. It's definitely very normal around here!"
Annie looked relieved and began to laugh happily.

Meanwhile, a couple of talks later, Annie came around again with some of the paste made up in a couple of containers.
"Give it a try and let me know your thoughts. I'll keep any significant notes also. I have to go as it's a busy day!" she said.
Annie smiled and rushed off to her car, waving cheerfully en route.
"I'll put some on my aching ankle," said Sarah.
"My eyes have felt a bit tired," responded Alyssia, "I'll try it out on my forehead."
"I'm sure we'll find many portions of our anatomy in need of TLC!" responded Kenny, and Karin chuckled.
But they all knew there would be more significant uses for it than the ones they had mentioned.

During that night a full moon shone down upon the Pistyll Rhaeadr valley. The upper parts of the waterfall received the brilliant silvery light, and the trees on the north side behind the chalets. Sarah awoke unexpectedly, feeling a strong compulsion to pick up the jar of paste and focus on what would be required. She then removed some of the concoction with her index finger,

asked inwardly that she could be allowed to know the deeper meaning of the properties that the amaranth held. She then applied the paste to her third eye, and could feel a tingling sensation. She then lay down and waited to see if anything else would occur. The tingling increased, and she began to see coloured lights swirling around. There was a pause, and she knew she had to ingest some of the amaranth tincture also, which she did. A flood of energy soared through her, and it felt as if the universe and she were connected, and the knowledge and wisdom of all the cultures on Earth and the Heavens were there to know, and were now a part of her.
'What a marvellous plant this is!' thought Sarah, 'we must share this with those who would understand.'

Next morning, Sarah told the others about her experience.
"Let's try it, girls!" stated Kenny, "but wait 'til I've been out for provisions!"
"Look! I can see some of the locals peering through the window!" cried Alyssia.
"Oh! Come in!" said Kenny, loudly.
The locals were the elementals, who filtered through the chalet walls, being of the next dimension, and cheerfully greeted everyone. They were Leannah, Garalph, Gadair and Kavanos, who were representatives of the fairies, gnomes, elves and fauns of the area.
"We've found out you've been using the paste, and wanted to talk to you about it!" explained Leannah, animatedly. "We were told by Jadeir that the amaranth paste was being made, as he'd been watching Annie."
"Oh, so he's been eavesdropping; might have known!" responded Kenny, with a mischievous grin.
Leannah and the others laughed merrily, and their laughter left a tinkling echo that resonated around the whole of Kenny and Karin's chalet.

Later that afternoon they were all in the living room of Kenny and Karin's chalet, Kenny and Karin having done their shopping.
"Should we all lie down after applying this paste?" asked Kenny, looking at Sarah, "you know, it may also work in sitting position."
"Possibly, Kenny, but I did find lying down the best," replied Sarah, "I could get some camping mats from our chalet."
"Or we could just go and lie on our own beds, easier!" responded Alyssia.
"I think it's nicer if we do it together initially," suggested Karin.

"Ok, I'll get the mats," said Sarah, and she darted off.

Once returned, with everything arranged on the living room floor, they applied the amaranth and lay down. Sarah felt the same tingling feeling, the coloured lights, and the heightened awareness that allowed her to feel linked between Heaven and Earth. The others felt it in the same way.

Suddenly they were out of their bodies, hovering above them. They all looked at each other, wondering what to do next.
"Let's go and visit the top of the waterfall!" said Alyssia.
In the next instance, the four of them were there, watching the afternoon sun catching the top of it. Alyssia looked through the aperture in the rock overhanging the top of the waterfall, to the valley below, then asked the others where they would like to go.
"What about the centre of the Earth?" suggested Kenny, "since I never went!"
"Good choice!" responded Karin.
"We agree too!" said Leannah and Garalph, who had speedily hovered into view.
The group laughed, and Leannah and Garalph joined in.
"Could you help us to get there, since we are in a different place these days?" asked Sarah.
"We thought you'd need some help!" replied the elementals, "take our hands!"
So they all did. Next minute they were pulled down behind the waterfall and deep into the ground, travelling down tunnels until they found a door with some carving upon it.
"Just knock and answer to whoever opens it," explained Garalph.
Sarah said she would knock, and as she did, the carving became animated, and asked her who the being is she knows in the centre of the Earth.
"Kundara," replied Sarah, calmly.
An emanation of peace suffused everyone, and the door opened, showing fiery light. Everyone stepped through and flew downwards, led by Leannah and Garalph, until a building could be seen. Then smiling faces. Sarah and Alyssia recognised them immediately.
"Kundara! Mimirmaré!" they cried.
"Welcome back, and welcome to your friends," Kundara and Mimirmaré spoke, "we thought you may return, and glad you did, as we have something for you to take back up to the surface."
They beckoned for them to follow, and they went into the Great Hall, and wandered through to a door at the far end. The room

was like an altar room, with a profound perfume that made everyone feel a deeper peace, and then realised it was amaranth.

"We've been using amaranth paste to gain a deeper insight on life," said Alyssia.

Kundara smiled knowingly, "we know, we can perceive what goes on above ground, but we don't pry, only know what's relevant to know!"

She went to the altar and picked up a large crystal and used it to open a wooden door, which was locked using crystal bolts. Inside the door was a book, which held information that the group knew would be valuable.

"Hold it in your hands and you will take the essence of the wisdom within you, which you will know over the coming days," advised Kundara.

They passed the book, one to another, slowly and meditatively. Each one of them felt something profound was entering them, and they all smiled to Kundara and Mimirmaré, and to Leannah and Garalph.

"I'm not sure of the contents yet, but I feel a strange sense of destiny, of sureness," said Kenny.

"I think that sums it up really well," agreed Sarah, and Karin and Alyssia affirmed it too.

"It will make you feel very sure," said Kundara.

"Now you must return, but you will be in our hearts always," commented Mimirmaré, wherever you may be."

Sarah had a strange inkling with those last few words of Mimirmaré. She looked at Alyssia, and caught her eye, Alyssia understood too. They all walked quietly out of the Hall, and then Kundara and Mimirmaré exchanged hugs with the group, and they left to return upwards through the fiery light, to the door, and then over the waterfall and back to their bodies lying on the floor. They slowly began to stir.

"Our journey to the centre of the Earth, magnificent!" said Kenny, happily.

"That book! I hope we shall know its contents well," commented Alyssia.

"We all have it, so we can help each other!" said Karin, reassuringly. "I'll put my channelling powers to good use."

"Yes, good, and some meditating," said Alyssia.

"The principles to have before embarking on acquiring this knowledge are, to be totally humble, non worldly ambitions, only wanting to be of selfless service to others. Then this information will come," stated Sarah, the next morning.

"Yes indeed, having meditated this morning already, I feel that the book contains the highest wisdom given in ancient cultures," responded Alyssia.

They all decided to meditate that morning, Alyssia and Sarah together in their chalet, and the other two in theirs, and compare notes afterwards.

Alyssia concentrated and immediately she saw a mass of greenery covering the planet and became immersed in it all, and could feel as if nature was pristine, pure and how it should be. Within it, man was able to live in harmony in those small villages she had seen on many occasions, when a mass of emerald green light almost blinded her with its brilliance, 'nature wants man to know and love it, and be a true part of it, instead of using it and immersing himself in technology and its derivatives so much', were the words that came strongly to her. Then she saw an image of an ancient crystal tool embedded in the ground above the waterfall. She looked at it closely, and pinpointed where it would be in order to obtain it, if that is what was required. She saw Leannah briefly saying it was meant to be found. Looking at the tool she could feel a timelessness there, and a goodness that simply shone from the tool. It was asking to be used, and once held by others, a deep peace would come to them, whether they understood the facts of esoterica or not.

"I saw this crystal at the waterfall that I have to find, Sarah," said Alyssia afterwards, and she gave Sarah all that she had perceived, including the greening of the land.

"How wonderful, I saw the same things, and that it would enhance our own inner feelings on what we brought back with us. That deep timeless peace that stands strong and silent, and unaffected by anything inharmonious," responded Sarah.

The four of them went to talk to the campsite owner, Jim, about what they had seen. He wanted to ensure they were careful in what they did to the land, and to let him see the results afterwards. The group borrowed a couple of trowels and approached the spot at the top of the waterfall. The ground, understandably, was hard, but Kenny managed to loosen it, digging down a couple of feet. Leannah appeared in their midst, and encouraged them to dig a bit more and slightly more at a diagonal, since she could see it plainly enough below ground. Kenny continued to remove the soil, then paused for breath.

"I can see something shining!" cried Sarah, who was gently scraping away some soil inside the hole. Everyone was there, peering in for a closer look.

"Look Kenny! It's definitely something there!" said Karin, excitedly.

Kenny resumed his digging, removing the soil around the object, to reveal the whole thing.

"It appears to be inside a case of some kind," remarked Alyssia.

"There! I've got it!" cried Kenny, "I can lift it out now."

Kenny prised the object out of the ground carefully, and lifted it up for all to see.

"What a lovely case," said Sarah, "it looks like orichalcum again."

Sure enough, it was made of that reddish gold metal, and needed coaxing to open. Leannah appeared again.

"Just sing a note you feel inspired to do, and it will open," she instructed.

The group did so, which turned out to be whatever came to mind spontaneously, and it was a cord.

Effortlessly, the case opened very slightly, and Kenny managed to get the lid to open a bit more. Enough to see the crystal inside.

"It needs a bit of oil on it to open it fully," said Kenny, "I'm sure our friend Jim will have some."

They were soon at Jim's door, having left the field as it was previously, and he provided the necessary oil.

"That's fascinating, I'd love to see it again when you have a spare moment," he said, "it certainly has some power, like an ancient grail that takes you back to some pristine origin that has been long forgotten."

"That sums it up just right, Jim!" responded Kenny.

Each of them meditated with the crystal tool, which had a two-inch wide clear quartz crystal, set in a short orichalcum, waisted handle, and was the length of the crystal, along with the amaranth paste. Sometimes they held group meditations in one of the chalets. They each agreed something was changing their perspective. Alyssia felt such a depth a love and peace in her heart that required stillness and constant concentration. She conferred with the others and they agreed it was happening to them also. They would include this new development in their talks, of which more were on the horizon.

They were soon back in Glastonbury for another talk. Sarah began to talk of her experience with the herbs.

"Now I shall tell you all about the seeds of amaranth paste that aided our concentration, and I want to give you a guided meditation and apply some of this paste. Those of you who wish to do this meditation, would you like to indicate this with a show of hands," explained Sarah.

A sea of hands rose into the air.

"Wonderful!" responded Sarah, "there are several pots of the paste. I'll give people at the row ends the pots, and please pass it along, having helped yourself to a small amount. Ideally, once everyone has some, please apply to your forehead, but do what is convenient."

Once everyone had the paste and applied it, Sarah led them into a peaceful state. Alyssia, Karin and Kenny had lit a number of candles in a large circle, surrounding the audience, along with herbs brought back from Astragandara, and were quietly walking around clockwise to ensure the incense permeated the audience area. Sarah then took out the crystal from Pistyll Rhaeadr, and spoke prayerfully. When Karin, Kenny and Alyssia had arranged themselves, so they were standing at the four points of the compass, with Sarah being the fourth. They all chanted in unison in the language of ancient Atlantean, and almost singing the words, the Atlantean that had been inherited faithfully from Lemuria. The crystal was passed around the perimeter of the circle, ensuring that its power permeated everyone in the room participating in the meditation. As everyone came to afterwards, the Oswestry group could see that inner glow beginning to radiate from people.

The organiser of the workshop wanted the group to come and give more of those meditations on a regular basis, perhaps go and live there, as she knew many people who would be interested, and to sell the paste as well.

"I think it's time we taught others to administer healing with all these herbs, and the paste," said Sarah.

"Agreed, we can have a series of workshops put into place," responded the organiser, "as soon as next weekend, will that be convenient?"

"Perfect!" replied Kenny.

The day arrived, and they brought in lots of the main herbs, paste, and Astragandaran herbs, and proceeded to talk about their uses, the journeys they went on to retrieve them, and how to use them. There was also a pile of their books for sale nearby.

As the last of that series of workshops drew to a close, and many Atlantean herb seeds and small plants distributed far and wide, the group wended back to Pistyll Rhaeadr.

"You know, I feel we have done everything possible we needed to do here," said Alyssia.

"I feel the same way, now that the third book is out, and dear old Plas Myrddin is well stocked with copies!" cried Kenny.

"Oh look! Annie's here!" said Alyssia, happily.

She pulled in and parked her car, then came over.

"Hello all!" she cried cheerfully, "look! I've picked up a newspaper today, and look what's in it!"

They all went into Karin and Kenny's chalet, and Kenny took the paper and began to read it out aloud to everyone.

"Plas Myrddin's latest selling point proved to be of great interest to a certain sector of the public. Their new trilogy about Atlantis talks of travel across time, rescuing caskets of spiritual value, and helping to redeem the cosmic order of life itself. Collaborated by four intriguing people, the public interest is ever growing stronger."

Kenny paused, and a look of astonishment came over his face, and he looked at Sarah.

"That's exactly what I got some time ago, Annie, when I looked at the well one morning," said Sarah, bringing out a piece of newspaper folded up in an envelope.

Annie looked at it, and curiously, the date was conveniently just above the article, shown as from last year.

"How strange!" remarked Annie, also astonished.

"Somehow, we knew this was coming," explained Sarah, "and we have to hand over everything to those we have taught, for it is our time to return, Annie."

Before that moment, Sarah hadn't known she would say that, but now she and the others knew their time on Earth was completed.

"You mean, returning to Atlantis? Or the other planets?" queried Annie.

"Astragandara and Verdamara," answered the group. "You and Jim can continue the work!" they explained, "the owner of the campsite, Annie!"

At that moment Jim appeared, and they showed the crystal to Jim and Annie, and handed it to them.

"You are now the keepers of the crystal and herbs and will soon be able to travel to Atlantis, watch for the signs," advised Kenny.

The familiar sound of a spaceship became apparent overhead. Zanadar appeared in their midst, and asked if they were ready. The group retrieved the belongings they wished to take, and then hugged Annie and Jim, and then were gone in a shaft of light. Jim took Annie's hand, and the crystal showered deep peace around them, and gave them the promise for a deep peace to enter into the world during the times ahead.

An Overall View of the Trilogy

The Atlantean trilogy could be seen as a fantasy story, or one of those Merlin-like tales that abound. It was channelled to me as a tale that evokes much about life outside the everyday world that we know. Its purpose is evocative and to inspire.

It talks of ancient times when temples were regarded with deep respect, for the priests were the guardians of their world and mentors of the populace. They understood how to use energy to benefit people, and the planet. They respected the sacred nature of life, and many beings shared their world. Unicorns, Pegasus', benign beings from other planets, and elementals constantly worked with them, who would also give advice and wisdom to temples.

All this would have taken place predominantly in the golden ages of the Atlantean culture, and their clairsentience, especially in the priesthood and priestess hood, would have been well developed.

This psychic power became so degenerated during the last kali ages at the end times of Atlantis, that a lot of gifts they had then, were abused, causing a lot of potency to be shut down. This, of course is why so much has been coming to light spiritually in recent times.

I have tried to show the contrasts between times periods, and how their use of technology is echoed in our present culture. At best, it was used with discrimination for their work and with spiritual intent, unlike the end times, when it was extensively used with materialistic intent, like today, to control the public.

In book 1, the clairsentient abilities becomes awakened in the people who enter the story and they travel to Atlantis to help find the caskets and bring that lost potency back into life.

In book 2, the Atlantean Codes enter the story, first brought to Atlantis from the Pleiades, but lost in time. They, like the caskets, have transformative powers and bring light to restore harmony along the star-ways, and for self-transformation.

Book 3 links the Garden of Eden on Earth to two other planets, Lemuria, the spirit world, and the centre of Earth. It aims to resolve and restore harmony on Earth, the Oswestry group bring back their wisdom from these places, including a visit into future times, and then give their insights to others.

All in all, the trilogy intends to show what wisdom these ancient civilisations had, another version of the age-old wisdom to bring inspiration.

Like the lady who wrote a number of books on ancient wisdom, Dion Fortune, some were fiction to evoke wisdom from an intuitive right-brained angle, and others were factual, to bring through information for the left brained side.

I think both story and factual information had equal validity, since, we don't always know everything that happened in ancient cultures, and so a bit of intuitive insightfulness can bring through information that wouldn't be possibly available via the intellect.

www.ingramcontent.com/pod-product-compliance
Lightning Source LLC
Chambersburg PA
CBHW061646040426
42446CB00010B/1597